World War II

A Beginner's Guide

ONEWORLD BEGINNER'S GUIDES combine an original, inventive, and engaging approach with expert analysis. Innovative and affordable, books in the series are perfect for anyone curious about the way the world works and the big ideas of our time.

aesthetics
africa
american politics
anarchism
animal behaviour
anthropology
anti-capitalism
aquinas
art
artificial intelligence
the baha'i faith
the beat generation
the bible
biodiversity
bioterror & biowarfare
the brain
british politics
the Buddha
cancer
censorship
christianity
civil liberties
classical music
climate change
cloning
the cold war
conservation
crimes against humanity
criminal psychology
critical thinking
daoism
democracy
descartes
dewey
dyslexia
energy

engineering
the english civil wars
the enlightenment
epistemology
the european union
evolution
evolutionary psychology
existentialism
fair trade
feminism
forensic science
french literature
the french revolution
genetics
global terrorism
hinduism
the history of medicine
history of science
homer
humanism
huxley
international relations
iran
islamic philosophy
the islamic veil
journalism
judaism
lacan
life in the universe
literary theory
machiavelli
mafia & organized crime
magic
marx
medieval philosophy
the middle east

modern slavery
NATO
the new testament
nietzsche
the northern ireland conflict
nutrition
oil
opera
the palestine–israeli conflict
particle physics
paul
philosophy
philosophy of mind
philosophy of religion
philosophy of science
planet earth
postmodernism
psychology
quantum physics
the qur'an
racism
reductionism
religion
renaissance art
the roman empire
the russian revolution
shakespeare
the small arms trade
sufism
the torah
the united nations
volcanoes

World War II
A Beginner's Guide

Christopher Catherwood

ONEWORLD

A Oneworld Paperback

Published by Oneworld Publications, 2014

Copyright © Christopher Catherwood 2014

The right of Christopher Catherwood to be identified as the Author
of this work has been asserted by him in accordance with
the Copyright, Designs and Patents Act 1988

ISBN 978-1-78074-510-7
eISBN 978-1-78074-511-4

Typeset by Siliconchips Services Ltd, UK
Printed and bound by
Nørhaven A/S, Denmark

Oneworld Publications
10 Bloomsbury Street
London WC1B 3SR
England

Stay up to date with the latest books,
special offers, and exclusive content from
Oneworld with our monthly newsletter

Sign up on our website
www.oneworld-publications.com

To

Woodall Okuykendall Berry Jr and Lacy Foster Paulette Jr

veterans of World War II

and to their wonderful niece, my wife Paulette

Contents

Contents

Introduction

Imagine eighty million people.

That is the latest agreed figure for the total number of deaths in World War II, from sources such as the Public Broadcasting Service in the USA and British writers such as Anthony Beevor. It is far higher than the originally agreed death toll of 55 million. Whichever way one looks, it is an extraordinary figure as it represents far more people than most nations today have people living in them.

The United Kingdom has 63 million inhabitants and the biggest US state, California, has 38 million. As the Netherlands has around 17 million inhabitants, the new consensus death count is the populations of the United Kingdom and the Netherlands combined, or just over twice the number of Californians. So imagine if all the British and Dutch were killed or if an earthquake wiped out the whole West Coast of the USA and Canada. And that would only approximate to the death toll of World War II.

We are familiar with some statistics, including that of the near six million Jews wiped out in the Holocaust. But some of the even greater genocides from the war may not be so familiar. Twenty-seven million Soviet citizens were wiped out in the four years 1941–5, and a full fifteen to seventeen million of those were civilian non-combatants. A fifth of the entire Soviet state of Belarus lost their lives. At least twenty million Chinese were killed and over six million Poles. Of the belligerent nations, the Japanese lost at least three million and perhaps as many as nine million ethnic Germans were killed.

But then compare the two main English-speaking participants, the United States and the United Kingdom, for which figures are probably more reliable. Some 418,000 Americans died, all but 1,700 being military. For Britain, the most recent count is 383,000 combat deaths and around 67,000 civilians who died in bombing raids and similar attacks.

When we think of the war, what picture comes to mind? Is it the Blitz in London? The story of how brave American troops landed in Normandy on D-Day? Both these images are wholly legitimate and probably an accurate representation of how two English-speaking nations experienced the conflict.

The death toll puts the carnage of the war into a very different perspective from the one familiar in Western countries. Fourteen percent of all Soviet citizens died, and 0.32% of Americans.

Television documentaries, such as those by Laurence Rees, have begun to show the war in its true light. However, for many of us this perspective will be wholly new. It is to explain the more recent revised way of thinking about World War II that is the main purpose of this book.

Furthermore, it is, as the title states, a *Beginner's Guide*. One of the most widely used university textbooks is Gerhard Weinberg's *A World at Arms*. It is a definitive work. It is also 1,178 pages long. To use a culinary example, it is a main course book. What we have in this book, therefore, is an appetiser, something to stimulate interest in World War II for non-specialists. By this I mean the keen amateurs who have not read the arcane expert literature, but who want a basic introduction on the foundation of which they can then dig deeper.

It is inevitable that in so short a book much has to be left out. This is a bird's-eye view of the war, written with the hope that someone wanting to know much more about particular details will now be inspired to follow up in depth about matters that could only be skirted over here. A Further Reading section is provided for this purpose.

Just to take two examples of what this book will consider: when did the war begin and what proportion of German troops fought the Allies in Western Europe as opposed to the conflict with the USSR on the Eastern Front?

It is said that a British actor realised that he needed to return home to the UK from Hollywood when his school-age daughter told him that World War II began in 1941. Of course, if you are American, then 1941 is the correct date of entry into the war – but for the British war broke out on 3 September 1939, over two years earlier.

However, that is an English-speaking perspective. For the USSR the war also began in 1941. The surprise twist comes in that for the Chinese, 1937 is actually a far more logical place to begin, a whole four years and more before Hitler invaded the Soviet Union. Therefore, as we shall see, when war began is itself an issue for debate.

Second, British people can be condescending – sometimes with good historical reason – about the Hollywood version of the past. The Enigma machine was smuggled to the UK by Poles and not by an American submarine, and there were as many British and Canadians fighting on the beaches on D-Day as Americans. While, therefore, a wonderful TV series such as *Band of Brothers* is accurate about the US experience it misses out almost altogether those equally courageous soldiers fighting alongside the Americans.

However, even television documentaries are now making the deeper truth about the war in Europe apparent: all the British, Canadian and US forces put together were fighting only fifteen percent of the German army. Fully eighty-five percent of the Wehrmacht was engaged not against us in the West, but against the Red Army. Compared to battles such as Kursk or Stalingrad, a battle such as Alamein merits hardly a mention.

It would seem unimaginable to a British person that Alamein would be unfamiliar to most other nationalities. Likewise, how many readers in the UK will be familiar with Midway, or Coral Sea, two of the most important and famous American victories in the Pacific?

This book is designed to introduce its readers to each other's greatest victories, to give as proper a balance as can be gained in where the real fighting was, and the battles that actually mattered. This is not to downplay the bravery of any army, especially that of my own country, the United Kingdom, whose solitary struggle from 1940–1 made long-term victory for the democracies possible at all. But it is to say that the major areas of struggle in World War II were the Soviets against Germany, and the Chinese and Americans against Japan. The contributions of other nations, such as Britain, Australia, Canada and India, while very far from irrelevant, were not central after the main conflict began in 1941. And, as we shall discover, logistics, especially that of the mighty industrial power of the USA, was every bit as important as the valour of the armies, navies and air forces in winning the war for the Allies.

1

The Origins of War and the Great Betrayal

Britain and other European countries are filled with memorials to a conflict described by those who built them as 'The Great War'. Sometimes the people of the town or university or whoever created the original plaque have added new names, for those killed between 1939–45.

Anyone who sees such monuments can notice that far more died in the first world war than in the second. These are of course military deaths, those killed in actual combat. What made World War II so much worse was the fact that millions of civilians were slaughtered in bombing raids, in deliberate genocide and in ways inconceivable before 1939.

Those who lived through what we now call World War I believed strongly that it was the 'War to End All Wars'– the last carnage on such a scale. People of the 1920s and 1930s could not conceive of the atrocities to come.

It is vital that we remember this. As Billy Wilder said, 'Hindsight is always twenty-twenty.' We see the years 1919–39 entirely and understandably through the prism of what happened in the six years that followed. It was a war that was truly on a scale unlike any other, genuinely global and with a death toll (of well over the 55 million guesstimate) that would have been inconceivable to the survivors of World War I. There is only one precedent for the number of civilians who died in World War II, namely the Thirty Years War of 1618–48. Perhaps only the ferocity and savagery of the Mongol Horde under Chinggis (or Genghis) Khan comes anywhere near the barbarity of the Japanese and Germans from 1937–45. In the 1920s, these Mongol invasions were a long way in the past.

It is very easy, therefore, to be wise after many events. Of few historical episodes is this more the case than with World War II. 'How could people not listen to Churchill,' we think, 'when you look at the Holocaust?'

THE HOLOCAUST

The murder of nearly six million innocent Jewish civilians during World War II has become the symbolic act of barbarism not just of that conflict but also arguably of all time. Unfortunately, events since the end of the war have put the Holocaust into a political perspective related to later and still current times. This means that their deaths are now seen more in the light of the present-day state of Israel than as a tragedy in its own right. In addition, other genocides have now been recognised. These include the murder of over a million Armenians in World War I and the death of tens of millions of Soviet citizens in World War II. The international concentration on the six million Jews has thus sadly been taken out of its own context and into a debate on whether murdered Jews have more right to be remembered than slaughtered Armenians or Poles.

This is deeply unfortunate as the death of six million innocent civilians is a tragedy, regardless of whether other equally blameless civilian groups were also murdered by the Nazis.

Furthermore, the Holocaust took place in distinct phases. Not everyone died in camps designed for extermination. The other description of the Holocaust is the Jewish word *shoah*. Historians divide the murders into the 'shoah by bullet' and the 'shoah by gas', with the death camps being the latter. German SS *Einsatzgruppen* (or killing squads) shot well over a million Jews in cold blood, the worst massacre being the butchery of 33,000 Jews in September 1941 at Babi Yar, a place near the Ukrainian capital of Kiev.

Much about the Holocaust remains a subject of debate, especially who decided what and when. But it seems that the notion of killing all eleven million Jews living in the whole of Europe arose when it seemed, briefly, in late 1941 as if the invasion of the USSR might be successful. Concentration camps, in which special category prisoners such as socialists, homosexuals and other anti-Nazi groups were interred, had existed from shortly after the Nazi takeover in 1933. When Poland was conquered in 1939 Jews were placed in small and enclosed areas in major cities, in ghettos, such as those that existed in Warsaw and Cracow. But this solution still created logistical problems for the Nazi occupying authorities, so the idea of total extermination of all Jews arose as mainstream policy.

The specific death camps for extermination – Treblinka, Auschwitz-Birkenau and others – began to be built from 1941 onwards, with gas chambers specifically constructed for the purpose of industrial-scale extermination. This policy was finalised at a meeting in a villa in Wannsee, a Berlin suburb, in January 1942. In charge was Reinhard Heydrich, number two in the SS hierarchy, but there were also diplomats from the German foreign office and similar bureaucrats from other ministries, for all of whom the death of eleven million people on purely racial grounds was entirely an administrative issue. Over a million Jews died at Auschwitz-Birkenau and some 800,000 at Treblinka.

Was the Holocaust unique? A reading of Hitler's work *Mein Kampf* and two decades of Nazi speeches suggests strongly that anti-Semitism was part of the core of Nazi DNA. The elimination of an entire human ethnic/religious group can be seen in the context of the desire also to exterminate, for example, all crippled or mentally defective people.

But anti-Semitism was also part of many fascist movements in Europe at that time. The massacre by Romanian troops of over fifty thousand Jews in the Black Sea port of Odessa in October 1941 shows that the Germans were not alone in their barbarous attitudes. (The pre-war Romanian League of the Archangel Michael was as violently anti-Semitic as the Nazi Party.) Many of the most enthusiastic SS death camp guards were Latvian or Ukrainian. Anti-Semitism was by no means a purely Germanic form of evil, and is a phenomenon with an ancient history throughout Europe.

Perhaps it is this quality of horror that makes the shoah unique. Tens of millions of civilians of all nationalities were cruelly butchered during World War II, but only the Jews were singled out for extermination on the grounds of ideological hatred and policy.

With the benefit of hindsight

Many have argued that in the great debates in the 1930s on how to treat Nazi Germany, Churchill was completely right to argue against the appeasement of Germany and vindicated by subsequent events such as the German seizure of the rump of Czechoslovakia in early 1939. But that is not how people saw it at the time. This can be illustrated by an interesting vignette from the conversation, just before D-Day, between a leading US official and Churchill's personal chief of staff, General Ismay. The Americans were, with good cause, troubled by the British lack of martial vigour for the impending invasion of Europe. Ismay's defence of his country's caution was to remind the Americans of the 57,000 British casualties on the first day of the Battle of the Somme in 1916. That the United Kingdom had been scarred by that experience was hardly surprising.

In retrospect, it would have been far better if the British army had been considerably larger in 1939 than was actually the case. This in itself is significant, because not even Churchill understood this. If one reads military historians such as the late Richard Holmes, and writers such as Gordon Corrigan, they all make the same point: that the army was too small. Churchill and others had a different view of what was needed, and since the UK only won the Battle of Britain in the skies by the narrowest of margins in 1940, it was as well that Churchill so zealously argued in the 1930s for an increase in the size of the Royal Air Force. But to fight a modern war, one needs soldiers and the right kind of equipment. From 1938–40, during the build-up to war and then its first phase, Britain arguably had far too few troops and nowhere near the right amount or kind of equipment to fight a continental war.

The chiefs of staff – the general staff of the army, and those of the navy and Royal Air Force – all instinctively knew much of this. But they had to deal with the politicians elected to govern by the British people, and in turn the government needed to be sensitive to public opinion in order to get elected. The key thing to remember is that after the carnage and trauma of the 'Great War' the last thing anyone wanted was another conflict on this scale. Churchill was not just a lone voice in the wilderness speaking against the obtuseness of lesser statesmen, but he was in reality going against the grain of the overwhelming mass of public opinion, not just in Britain but also in what were then the key Dominion nations such as Canada and Australia.

Furthermore, Britain was an Asian power as well as a European one. Until the 1970s, Britain had an entire fleet in the Pacific, based in Singapore. It also had extensive colonial possessions in what is now Malaysia. But the 'Jewel in the Crown' was the British Raj, which comprised what became India and Pakistan in 1947 (and thence Bangladesh later in 1971). This was a vast empire, richer than that of any other European country, and was at the heart of all the military and naval calculations made by the British government and by the chiefs of staff.

All that transpired between 1919–39 can be interpreted in this light. So, too, can much of what happened during the war. The generals of World War II were the lieutenants and captains of World War I. It could be argued that after the trauma of Flanders, they never shook off the survivors' guilt for living when so many of their comrades did not. Furthermore, as Max Hastings often reminds us, Britons are not by nature a martial race. 'Never again' is a potent rallying cry and it was one that was heard time and again in the twenty years between the two wars.

The main consequence of this was the virtual denuding of the victorious British Army after 1919, and thus of that country's ability to fight. Since time immemorial Britain had been a predominantly naval power. We can be profoundly thankful that in 1939 the Royal Navy was still powerful enough to protect the nation's shores. From conscription in 1916 until demobilisation three years later, the United Kingdom had gone against the grain and deployed a massive army on continental European soil, something that had not happened upon such a scale even in the Napoleonic wars.

The winners lose the way: the consequences of disarmament

But with victory Britain reverted to its old ways. The army was more an instrument of colonial power, as it had been for most of the nineteenth century, than a modern weapon to be deployed in Europe against a major power. Britain may have invented the tank (something in which Churchill played a key role as First Lord of the Admiralty and later as Minister of Munitions), but thereafter it was as if the Great War was an aberration in the nation's military history, never to be repeated.

As for the USA, its retreat into isolation is so famous as not to need much elaboration. Not so well known is the fact that as late as 1940 the US Army was no bigger than that of Belgium. But in the twenty years between 1919–39, the USA, however powerful economically, was a military minnow. Many ordinary Americans remained isolationist, and to them the very notion of a large peacetime army was anathema. The fact that even as far into the war against Hitler as the November 1940 presidential election, Roosevelt had to campaign on staying neutral or lose the White House, tells us all that we need to know about what the USA could or could not do in global affairs.

Both in moral terms and with the hindsight of 1937–45 (and perhaps with that of 1941–5 in particular) it is doubtful that much could have been done to stop Hitler and the Japanese in a way that would either have prevented the conflict altogether or lessened it considerably when it came. That, however, is not how people at the time saw it. As we shall see, it was not really until Hitler's seizure of the rump of Czechoslovakia in March 1939 that most British and Dominion (Canadian, etc.) people saw that war might be necessary, let alone inevitable. Even today there are mavericks in both Britain and the USA who still argue that isolation from continental Europe was the better option, however extraordinary such views might seem to most of us in the light of the Third Reich's barbarity.

The other issue that confuses the origins of World War II is that so many people in the West felt that the Germans had been unfairly treated in 1919. Compared to the total destruction of the country in 1945, Germany had in fact been let off rather lightly, but this again is to use a degree of hindsight unknown back in the 1920s and 1930s. Reparations soon came to be perceived as unjust, linked as it was to the concept that Germany alone had started war in 1914. As the cause of war had been the murder of an Austrian archduke, many rejected so simple an interpretation.

Since US president Woodrow Wilson had argued between 1917–19 for self-determination, it also seemed inequitable to most people that Germans should be denied what had been granted to other people. For example, Austria, while ethnically German, was not allowed to unite with Germany, thus negating Wilson's grant of self-determination to Poles, Czechs and other ethnic groups. When Hitler, therefore, began to rant against the Diktat of Versailles and demand renegotiation, he was asking for something that many in the West felt was only fair and Germany's due.

The debate: was it the Third Reich or simply Germany?

One of the major historical controversies of the 1960s was whether or not the Third Reich was simply Germany, a nation state like any other, or something altogether more evil and dangerous. Today most of us would argue that a country led by Hitler and one that passionately supported the philosophy and practices of Nazism deserved nothing at all. But we have to remember that in the 1920s, under the moderate conservative politician Gustav Stresemann, Germany was seen as rehabilitating itself among the civilised nations (and Stresemann won no less than the Nobel Peace Prize for German–French reconciliation in 1926). When Germany under his leadership signed the Kellogg–Briand Pact of 1928, renouncing all recourse to war, most people would have thought that the era of German aggression was over and that peace would prevail. That very year, the Nazis, a small and nationally insignificant minor party, won a mere 2.6% of the national vote.

We should also remember that in World War I Japan and Italy were on the side of Britain, France and the USA, and thus not perceived at all as being in the enemy camp.

What changed everything was the Great Depression. In September 1930, the Nazis won 18.25% of the national vote. In the July 1932 elections they scored their greatest electoral triumph, gaining 37.27%. It is usually forgotten that in the November 1932 contest, the Nazis actually lost votes and seats in the Reichstag, going down over 4% to 33.09%.

Hitler was made chancellor of Germany in January 1933 in what must rank as one of the most foolish moves in the history of politics. The German conservatives who put him in the post thought that they could control him by making him what they felt would be a puppet chancellor. This is important to remember. While the Nazis were now a major political force in their own right, they were never elected to power by democratic mandate. Perhaps as a result of this, it took a while for Hitler to consolidate his power. But in 1934, his grip became stronger when he gained the presidency and also the loyalty of the Wehrmacht, the German army, after purging his Nazi Party rivals in the SA, or Sturmabteilung, the 'Stormtroopers'. This last group saw itself as a source of potential independent power, and was thus perceived as a possible threat not just by Hitler but by the army as well.

Germany, Italy and Japan: revisionist powers?

Much discussion about the origins of World War II has been in terms of the three 'revisionist' powers: Germany, Italy and Japan, nations who wanted to revise the post-1919 global settlement made in Paris. This is all historically valid, since each of the three nations had various grievances that they felt the democracies had not resolved. (Any semblance of democracy in Italy had vanished in the 1920s, and it was always shaky in Japan especially as the power of the army and navy grew greater.)

In the case of Japan and Italy, a major factor in switching sides from being on the side of Britain and the USA in 1919 to being revisionist by the 1930s was the desire for imperialist expansion. Here one has to admit that the Western democracies were guilty of double standards. Today most people regard colonialism and imperialism as wrong, whatever their politics, and especially the racist ideology upon which it is based. But in the nineteenth century, in the 'Scramble for Africa' Britain, France and Germany carved up much of that continent. This, added to earlier colonial holdings of the British, Dutch and French, had created vast empires in Asia.

In the twenty-first century, many would argue that the British conquest of India was no different in kind from the Japanese desire to colonise first Manchuria (a region of China) and then, after 1937, the rest of the country. What is the difference between Britain conquering the lands of present-day Nigeria in the 1890s and Mussolini ordering the invasion of Ethiopia some four decades later? Now we would say that all such acts are wrong. But in the 1930s, Churchill was zealously defending British rule in India while at the same time denouncing German imperial aims in Europe.

When the Japanese began their campaigns of conquest in 1941 they seized many countries that were Asian nations ruled over by Europeans, an irony lost on many Western countries but certainly not on the indigenous peoples who had simply swapped one foreign ruler for another. Today we can criticise all such imperialism as morally unacceptable, but in the 1930s it was not quite so simple. The large-scale brutality of Japan showed millions of their fellow Asians that the Japanese were if anything far more repressive than the light-touch Europeans. But with Italy we should not forget that Mussolini did not finally side militarily with Hitler until the fall of France – the 'appeasement' of Italy, while morally reprehensible, was a policy that very nearly succeeded.

But being nice to Hitler, however plausible his pleas for the reunification of all ethnic Germans into a single country, was another matter altogether. This is why we ought to consider the policy of the democracies towards Germany as being in a different category, since the true nature of the Nazi regime was apparent early on. Mussolini might have been an unpleasant piece of work, but nothing in Italy compared to the concentration camps, built from the outset of the Third Reich, or the mass killing of the SA stormtroopers in 1934, when Hitler and the army colluded to kill the SA leadership. The latter, under their leader Ernst Röhm were perceived by Hitler to be a source of rival leadership within the Nazi party. Even without hindsight it was surely apparent that Nazi Germany was operating on an altogether different scale of brutality from Italian fascism.

However, the democracies had demilitarised on a massive scale back in the 1920s, confident that global and industrial-scale war would never return. By the time Hitler was in power in 1933, the world economy had also collapsed, and the prosperity that would have been needed to rebuild vast armies, navies and air forces to deal with the menace now posed was simply no longer there. Pacifism was deeply ingrained in the electorates of the Western democracies, since everyone had a brother or father or friend who had died in World War I.

Remember, too, that the political left, while resolutely anti-fascist, was equally opposed to rearmament, and believed strongly instead in the supposed powers of that paper tiger, the League of Nations. The League had been created by Wilsonian idealism, but ironically the USA did not join. It was a Great Power that had retreated not just from Europe but also from wielding power anywhere in the world. Germany was admitted to the League for good behaviour in 1926 but left as soon as Hitler gained power, and the USSR was admitted as late as 1934. It was all very easy to oppose Hitler, and morally the right thing to do; but with no weapons and a League of Nations which had no teeth, effective opposition to the growing threat of Nazi Germany was therefore, to all intents and purposes, non-existent.

In looking at the many reasons for the unexpected fall of France in 1940, we should not forget the complete suspicion of Communism among the ruling classes of Western Europe (and almost certainly of the USA as well). The Communist attempts at revolution in Germany and Hungary in 1919 had failed but they had scared Europe's elites witless. Whatever Hitler may or may not be (and the same argument can be applied to Mussolini and later to Franco), he and they were not Communists. This considerably distorted the view of Nazi Germany, and made all the difference when the threat posed by Hitler entered a new dimension in 1938, the year that the countdown to war began in earnest.

The naval treaty: Britain betrays Versailles

Versailles was opposed not just by the overtly revisionist powers. Even the key signatories – Britain, France and Italy – were now all to take significant actions that were to undermine the basis of the post-war settlement.

Most historians, inspired by Winston Churchill's own view of events, feel that the last chance that the West European governments had to prevent Hitler and thereby stop what became the new world war was in March 1936. At this time, German troops reoccupied the Rhineland, the border area with France that had been specifically demilitarised by the Treaty of Versailles in 1919. If only we had halted him then, the traditional argument goes, we would never have had the conflict that broke out in September 1939.

Nevertheless, Hitler was occupying what was indisputably German territory (the argument we will explore later of the so-called appeasers) but also he was able to do so with a newly expanded army, the Wehrmacht.

One might argue that the real betrayal was by Britain in 1935, the year before the occupation of the Rhineland. Hitler needed an army for his expansion plans, and an effective air force, the Luftwaffe, as well as a fully operational submarine fleet of U-boats. The army also needed tanks, or panzers. All of these had been expressly forbidden by the Treaty of Versailles, and without them Hitler would not have been able to conquer anywhere, let alone most of continental Europe in 1940 and the western USSR in 1941.

In order to start the process of fulfilling his plans, Hitler denounced the Versailles restrictions in March 1935. France and Britain would have been fully entitled to ask him to cancel his decision, but they did nothing.

Britain and France signed an agreement with Mussolini's Italy in the Italian town of Stresa in April 1935. This particular action, that created a tripartite 'Stresa Front' was not binding militarily but signalled the anxiety that the three former World War I allies had about the rise and potential threat of Nazi Germany since 1933. Italy had gained Austrian territory in the Tyrol in 1919 and so consequently had reason to fear a desire by Hitler to claim that ethnically German part of Italy back for the Third Reich.

Mussolini was no democrat, however. Although these three countries had been allies in World War I, Italy had taken a very different turn, in becoming a fascist state in the 1920s. Ideologically, therefore, this agreement was a strange one.

Then in June 1935, the British government did something extraordinary. They signed the Anglo-German Naval Agreement that stipulated that so long as the German navy did not exceed thirty-five percent of the size of the Royal Navy, Germany would be allowed to expand its fleet.

This was a distinct undermining of the entire Versailles settlement, and Britain was entirely responsible for it. Not only had they failed to prevent German military expansion in clear breach of the treaty but they were now, in effect, endorsing it. This was a far worse offence than failure to act in March 1936, since in June 1935 the British had for all intents and purposes signalled to Hitler that they did not mind his active revisionist approach to Versailles and the entire settlement upon which the world had been based since 1919. The Rhineland debacle was the symptom of a disease that had already affected the British rather than the cause itself.

Looking to two other European powers, France and the Soviet Union had signed a friendship pact in May 1935. This reflected a similar agreement to the one that tsarist Russia had signed with the French in the late nineteenth century. It was a natural alliance, the two countries troubled by the rise of German militarism, and while Germany and the USSR no longer had a common border, with Poland coming in between since 1919, it was a friendship that made strategic sense.

Britain's deal with Germany annoyed the French, and France's deal with the USSR irritated the British. Both events seriously angered Mussolini's Italy, which had no love for the Soviet Union and which had reasons to fear German territorial expansion.

The anti-German Stresa Front was thus dead in the water soon after signature, and Italy would soon embark on imperial adventures. The Italians had been convincingly defeated by Abyssinia in 1896 and Mussolini wanted revenge. In the autumn of 1935, therefore, he launched an attack on Abyssinia. It was a battle of twentieth-century technology versus that of a much earlier age.

The British, however, were not happy at the conquest of Ethiopia since the latter was a sovereign independent nation that was a full member of the League of Nations. Britain as a major imperial power was being wholly hypocritical, since the kingdoms in what became Nigeria only thirty to forty years before were as sovereign and independent in the nineteenth century as Ethiopia was in 1935. But those conquests, made in the late Victorian era, had been carried out in the swansong of the age of European conquest and expansion, and by the 1930s such behaviour was no longer acceptable. Britain was able to engineer sanctions against Italy, which had the inevitable effect of pushing Mussolini away from Italy's former allies into the arms of his fellow dictator, Adolf Hitler.

Nevertheless, the phantom of resurrecting the Stresa Front persisted in British minds for years, even down to May 1940 when Lord Halifax, then foreign secretary, raised Italian mediation as a way of rescuing Britain from invasion. But after 1935 it was surely a pure chimera, as events were to show.

Thanks to British pusillanimity Hitler was now able to start rearming with a vengeance. Churchill stood up to the British government, but as he had ruined his credibility by his zealous opposition to independence for India, his was a voice in the wilderness. The Labour Party was equally against Fascism, but in their case their credibility was affected by the fact that they also opposed rearmament, which was the opposite of what Britain needed.

In 1931, the king of Spain had been overthrown along with the quasi-military regime that he supported and Spain became a republic. But many in the military never accepted democratic change and feared the rise of the political left that democracy had empowered. In 1936, a group of officers, led by General Francisco Franco, invaded the mainland from Spanish North Africa and began three years of bloodthirsty civil war.

This Spanish conflict, from 1936–39, can be interpreted as a dry run for the global war that followed. Germany and Italy ignored the League of Nations' boycott and decided to back Franco. Italy sent troops and the Germans their infant air force, the Luftwaffe. Britain and France insisted on full neutrality and on an arms embargo, but this did not stop thousands of idealistic young Britons, Americans and Frenchmen and Frenchwomen from enlisting in what were called the International Brigades, armed divisions of volunteer soldiers joining up from around the world to try to defend the republic against Franco's Nationalist forces. Since the democracies kept the boycott and the dictatorships did not, this inevitably gave the rebels a military advantage over the republic.

Spain became the cause celebre of a whole generation, though the perceptive, such as George Orwell in *Homage to Catalonia*, came sadly to understand that the effective Communist takeover of the republican side meant that in reality the vicious conflict ended up with one totalitarian ideology pitted against another. Franco was a cruel dictator who slaughtered thousands

THE LESSONS OF HISTORY

The Foreign Office historian Gill Bennett, in her book *Six Moments of Crisis*, makes the excellent point that while it is always vital for politicians to learn from the past, nevertheless, sometimes they learn the wrong lessons from historical events.

Of few other episodes is this more true than the Munich crisis of autumn 1938. 'Appeasement' has become a dirty word. Ever since Churchill was proved right over Munich in 1939–40, political leaders have been terrified of repeating Chamberlain's mistake.

In 1956, Anthony Eden (who had resigned as foreign secretary in February 1938 to oppose appeasement) was prime minister and, seeing the Egyptian leader Colonel Nasser as a latter-day Mussolini, connived together with France and Israel to invade the Suez Canal, provoking one of the most disastrous episodes in the history of British foreign policy.

The war in Iraq in 2003 is probably still too controversial and recent to use as an example here. Yet it is certain that, once again, politicians decided that to 'appease' Saddam was wrong, and that the only action to take was to launch a war to remove him from power in clear distinction from the failure of Britain and France to do the same with Hitler back in 1938.

But whatever one's views on Suez or Iraq or any other major foreign policy imbroglio, it is almost certain that the events at Munich bore little if any similarity to the very different situations with which politicians were confronted decades later.

Munich shows that to betray an ally or let a democracy be crushed by a dictator is a terrible thing. Yet if one thinks of a more exact parallel – say Hungary in 1956 or Czechoslovakia in 1968 – there is little doubt that for the West to have come to the aid of either country during those crises could have triggered a third world war and nuclear Armageddon, consequences infinitely more dire than those that actually happened in 1939.

So politicians should always be aware of the past, rather than suffering from what Cambridge historian Christopher Andrew nicknames 'Historical Attention Deficit Disorder'. But the lessons should be the right ones.

of entirely innocent civilians, but Stalin's friends in Spain, including the future Yugoslav leader Josip Broz Tito, were not exactly virtuous either.

Appeasement: the debate continues ever onwards

The years 1937–38 is a period of history about which historians and many others remain profoundly divided well over three-quarters of a century after the events in question. The appeasement policy of the British government proved, in essence, to consist of being nice to Hitler, by giving him the things that seemed reasonable, while beginning *slowly* to build up Britain's armaments from the denuded state into which they had fallen after World War I. The following quotation from a speech by Neville Chamberlain in July 1938 shows the attitude of the appeasers in Britain:

> How horrible, fantastic, incredible it is that we should be digging trenches and trying on gas-masks here because of a quarrel in a far away country between people of whom we know nothing. It seems still more impossible that a quarrel which has already been settled in principle should be the subject of war.

This statement is all the more fantastic because the 'far away country', Czechoslovakia, is in Central Europe, hardly far beyond British reach.

Even today this policy of appeasement remains unswervingly as controversial as it did both at the time and in all the political and historical debates ever since. Much of the debate was set in motion by Winston Churchill, not just by his oratory in denouncing the policy, but in his espousal of the 'Guilty Men' thesis (of left-wing journalist and later politician Michael Foot) which argued that Britain could and should have acted otherwise. Churchill's memoirs, which he branded as a factual account, the six-volume *The History of the Second World War*, were not so much an objective history as a partisan defence of his actions during the conflict. Ever since, soldiers, historians and others have waged their own written wars on whether or not his interpretation was correct.

Chamberlain soon found friends among revisionist historians, writing in the 1960s. Since the secret government documents of the 1930s became declassified, those interested to find out for themselves began to discover not just what the politicians of the time actually thought and wrote but, crucially, also the thoughts of diplomats and soldiers, airmen and sailors who advised them and were critical in determining policy. In particular, books by historian John Charmley came passionately to Chamberlain's aid. This initiated a process by which Churchill ended up for some not as the hero but as the villain who threw away the British Empire. Churchill famously believed in victory whatever the cost. His decision to fight bankrupted Britain by 1945.

According to the new view, Churchill thereby ended decades (if not centuries) of Britain's global predominance, ceding supremacy to the post-war superpowers, the USA and the USSR. By contrast, the new interpretation argued, appeasement would have kept Britain out of the war. The British Empire would not have gone bankrupt in self-defence and the USA would thus not have replaced the United Kingdom as the global superpower in 1945.

As expected, a reaction brought a counter-reaction. Historians such as the Canadian Michael Jabara Carley (in his powerful *1939 And The Alliance That Never Was* and British academic Evan Mawdsley (in his convincing *World War II*) brought us almost full circle, to what Carley calls a 'post-revisionist' position.

For those who prefer simple narrative history all this might seem slightly arcane. But no history is written simply out of the blue, without some kind of conceptual framework behind it, and of no conflict is this more true than the origins and story of World War II.

Czechoslovakia: betraying a great democracy

The crisis over Hitler's desire to absorb into the Third Reich the ethnically German areas of Czechoslovakia climaxed at a conference between Germany, Britain, France and Italy in September

1938 in Munich, and ever since then 'Munich' has become like a swearword, an expression used by politicians as the reason why they will never surrender on a particular policy. In fact, the crisis had brewed all year, and had existed long before Hitler made use of it.

Czechoslovakia was one of the many artificial states created by the victorious allies in 1919. Yugoslavia, which also no longer exists, was another. Self-determination lay at the heart of Woodrow Wilson's new countries, but unfortunately many of these nations contained several nationalities whose goals conflicted with each other. Czechoslovakia had not just Czechs and Slovaks at its core, but also large Hungarian and Polish minorities and, most crucially, ethnic Germans in all its border regions, who had hitherto been part of the German-dominated Hapsburg Empire that vanished in 1918.

This would not have mattered so much but for the fact that the overwhelming preponderance of Czech military defences was in this very region: the Sudeten mountains or Sudetenland. In March 1938, Germany had invaded and successfully incorporated Austria into the Third Reich – to the massive joy of almost all but the Jewish minority. This was Anschluss, a union of Germany and Austria that had been specifically forbidden by the post-war treaties in 1919. But as it seemed at the time that one group of ethnic Germans was happy at joining another, Western governments never thought through the implications.

However, the Czechs fully understood the ramifications – the Czech end of the country was now surrounded on three sides by the Third Reich. Hitler next demanded through his Sudeten German stooge Heinlein that the Sudetenland be reunited with the Reich. This would at a stroke have removed all Czechoslovakia's defences from German invasion and also put the Skoda works, the most advanced munitions factory in Europe (if not the world at that time), dangerously close to Third Reich territory.

Hitler ratcheted up the tension. But rather than resist him and protect Czechoslovakia, the one genuine pluralist democracy in Central Europe, France dithered and let the initiative pass to Britain, whose government was determined not to have war. Space does not permit all the ins and outs of the summer of 1938, but by September 1938, at a conference brokered by Mussolini in Munich, Britain and France signed away all the Sudetenland to Hitler, giving him at a stroke of Chamberlain's pen all the German demands.

Czechoslovakia was not permitted to come to the conference that arranged its dismemberment, a disgrace which Churchill rightly proclaimed as an unmitigated defeat in one of his most powerful orations to the House of Commons. Equally significant, nor was the USSR invited. The Soviet Union was, as France was supposed to have been, a guarantor of Czechoslovak independence. At the time, Chamberlain was regarded as a hero, the man who had won 'peace in our time'. Ecstatic, enthusiastic crowds greeted Chamberlain back in Britain, a fact that, after his fall in 1940 has mainly been forgotten.

Was appeasement in fact the disaster that Churchill thought in 1938? Let us look as dispassionately as possible at the arguments, and in particular at the Czechoslovak crisis of 1938 upon which all the arguments hinge either way. And one thing to add here – in the 1940s when Churchill put his case, and in the 1960s when the revisionists put theirs, the Soviet archives were hermetically sealed. Today, with historians able to access many of them, it seems inconceivable that we could have such major arguments without knowing exactly what Stalin and the USSR were thinking, since the Soviet role was absolutely central to all that took place. But for over forty years that was indeed the case. Now that the archives are open, people have realised in reading them what really happened in the 1930s and why. This new perspective has restored the USSR to its correct role as pivotal to the outcome.

Chamberlain might have had a profound distrust of the Soviets, as he privately told his family, and Churchill might have jettisoned two decades of hatred of Communism to advocate an anti-Hitler alliance, but ultimately it is what Stalin thought that made all the difference, whether the British recognised that or not. With the key archives recently available, history can only now at last be written properly. Stalin felt that the anti-fascist cause had been betrayed by Britain and France. His new mistrust of the West was soon to have dire consequences.

So perhaps the real disaster of Munich was that it created the chain of events that led ultimately to the Nazi–Soviet Pact of August 1939. In this agreement the USSR decided to stay neutral in any war that Germany had with Western powers and, in secret annexes, carved Poland in two which gave the USSR predominance in the Baltic states, three countries that had escaped Russian rule in 1917–18. This gave Hitler carte blanche to invade Western Europe as well as the part of Poland allocated to him, in the sure knowledge that he would only have to fight a single front war.

THE PACT THAT CHANGED HISTORY (AND STILL DOES...)

The Molotov–Ribbentrop Pact, sometimes known as the Nazi–Soviet Pact, was signed on 23 August 1939. Not only did it change the nature of the whole war, but it is also a treaty that still makes a difference to the world we inhabit in the twenty-first century. For example, it changed borders with ramifications for who lives in which city.

Take a town called Lviv, one of the major cities of Ukraine and a place that has existed for nearly eight hundred years. But that is its recent name; from 1349–1772 and again from 1918–39 it was an indisputably Polish city (and with a large Jewish minority). From 1772–1918 it was called Lemberg, a city of the Hapsburg-ruled Kingdom of Galicia. In 1945, Roosevelt and Churchill wanted it to be returned to Poland. Stalin refused, and it is a Ukrainian city to this day.

In the West we have always thought that World War II was a 'good war', a moral crusade against tyranny, Japanese imperialism and European fascism. Tell that to a Pole...

Historical discussion about the Molotov–Ribbentrop Pact has been mainly in relation to its short-term impact on events in 1939–40. Its non-aggression agreement meant that Hitler and Stalin were able to carve up Central Europe, and then in 1940 Germany could launch its blitzkrieg, or 'lightning war' against Western Europe in the knowledge that it would only have to fight a war on their Western Front.

The Japanese were appalled, and their government resigned. We talk about the 'Axis Powers' of Germany, Italy and Japan, but in practice the amount of genuine consultation between them, especially between the Third Reich and Japan, was not great, as Hitler's agreement in August 1939 demonstrates. Germany and Japan would later become allies. But the Japanese had been given a pause for thought. As a consequence, they now realised that the idea of a German–Japanese two-front invasion of the USSR was off the agenda. Coupled with Japan's defeat by the Red Army that month near the Mongolian and Chinese border at Nomonhan (Kalkhin Gol), this changed the whole direction of the war, as the next chapter will explain.

If that is true, this would mean that Hitler's decision was one of the very worst of the war. It might have bought him time and the ability to conquer Western Europe, but it meant that by 1941 he would not get Japanese help against the USSR. While I will argue that *Barbarossa*, the German invasion of the USSR, was almost certainly doomed from the beginning, the fact that Stalin only had to fight a one-front war, safe from Japanese attack, made the critical difference to eventual Allied victory. The sense of betrayal Japan suffered over Molotov–Ribbentrop was to prove fatal to any chance that the Third Reich might have had of victory over the USSR, and thus of winning the war itself.

Did Munich give Hitler time to rearm as well?

Much academic blood has been spilled over whether or not Munich was a savage betrayal – which it surely was in any moral sense – or whether it was a timely agreement that bought the Allies vital time to rearm against Hitler. Here the revisionist and post-revisionist camps we saw earlier have been especially busy for well over seventy years, starting with Churchill's own memoirs and then coming into historical debate as the archives slowly opened.

Had the Czechs been able to resist a German attack in 1938, Nazi generals later admitted that they would have had a very hard time dealing with the powerful defensive lines. Opinion is still open on what the USSR could have done. The Poles, who had seized much Soviet territory in 1919, would never have allowed Red Army troops to enter their soil, and indeed in 1938 Poland equally betrayed the Czechs by taking a chunk of territory from them, a fact also often forgotten.

This is one of the famous what-ifs of history because, while the delay until September 1939 gave the British and French time to rearm, it also gave the same amount of extra rearmament time to the Germans. Furthermore, in March 1939, Hitler betrayed Britain and France by invading the rump of what was left of Czechoslovakia – he took Bohemia and Moravia. Slovakia became a German puppet state and much of the rest of the country went to the Hungarians (and the Ruthenian part to Stalin in 1945). All the equipment of the once-formidable Czechoslovak army went to the Third Reich, and so when France was invaded in 1940 much of the equipment used to defeat the French was Czech-made, all of which would have been on the side of the Allies in 1938 had things gone differently.

Ultimately, it is hard to know what might have happened. But we do now know what the Soviets decided. Stalin went from trying to build an anti-fascist coalition with his Jewish foreign

JOSEF STALIN, 1879–1953

Joseph Stalin (born Dzhugashvili) was the effective dictator and leader of the Soviet Union from 1930–53 and thus throughout the war.

Originally a Georgian, he transformed from a seminary student to active Bolshevik revolutionary, who played a key and unsuccessful role as a Soviet commissar in the Russo–Polish war up to 1920. By 1924, he was already climbing up the Communist Party ladder, and he was its boss and thus ruler of the USSR by 1930.

As recent writers from Laurence Rees to Timothy Snyder have shown, Stalin became a mass-murderer on an epic scale not seen since the Mongols and Tamerlane centuries before. During his time as leader, over eighteen million mainly innocent people were incarcerated in the gulag – the Soviet concentration camp system – and millions were butchered or starved to death in the Great Purge and Great Famine of the 1930s.

Yet it was the infamous Nazi–Soviet Pact of August 1939, in which Germany and the USSR carved up Poland and other parts of Central/Eastern Europe that made Hitler's blitzkrieg on the rest of Europe possible and World War II inevitable. The Soviet Union was lucky to emerge unconquered in 1941, but Stalin emerged victorious, able to compel his Western allies to allow him to keep his ill-gotten gains of 1939.

After 1941, in being allied with someone as monstrous as Stalin, the Allies were in league with a dictator as barbaric as Hitler, albeit of a different kind – ideologically not racially motivated. Not until 1989 would the peoples of Poland and similar countries be finally liberated from foreign tyranny.

minister Litvinov, to doing a deal with Hitler, with his new (and ethnically Russian) foreign minister Molotov. And surely, by any account, that was a setback for the West since Litvinov had been a supporter of uniting with the West against the Third Reich.

However immoral the betrayal of Czechoslovakia was in 1938, most British and Dominion opinion was against going to war. Therefore, while Churchill was morally absolutely right, and possibly militarily correct as well, perhaps it was better to have postponed the major war in Europe until Britain was at least internally united and mentally prepared. But surely it was a moral tragedy, and it made the war, when it happened, far worse than would otherwise have been the case, and certainly at terms far more disadvantageous to Britain. Had Hitler been obliged to fight a two-front war in 1939, the outcome of that year would have been very different, and not to his advantage.

2

Wars in Faraway Places: The War in China and in Europe 1937–40

World War II began by mistake, and not in Europe. On 7 July 1937, at a place near the then former Chinese capital of Beijing, at the Marco Polo Bridge, a Japanese soldier temporarily went missing. Fighting ensued, and what was originally intended as a peaceful military manoeuvre escalated into a fire-fight between Japanese troops and Chinese forces loyal to the Guomindang Nationalist Government, led by Chiang Kai-shek.

As one historian, Evan Mawdsley, has pointed out, the Japanese troops, who had been in occupation of Manchuria since 1931, were in fact 'training for a war against the USSR, not against China'. So what now happened was a world war by mistake, and not at all the one that many of the Japanese hawks intended. So angry were the Nationalist Chinese at what they felt was Japan's fiercely aggressive attitude at the bridge that they sent divisions to support the warlord in charge of the area around Beijing. This in turn led the new Japanese government under Prince Konoe to send three divisions of their own to reinforce their army near Beijing. This move was successful – the Japanese Kwantung army seized the old capital by the end of the month, and war began.

This was a war with no declared beginning. The Japanese persisted in referring to it as the 'China Incident'. But it was war all the same. So by 1937 Japan was in a conflict with China that was to cost the latter country over twenty million deaths, as we saw in the Introduction. Now the Japanese war of aggression extended to the whole of China and not just to the areas of the northeast it had seized in 1931. For Japan and China, therefore, there was continuity in the conflict, which broadened out in 1941 and continued until 1945. Today, we are just beginning to remember the 27 million Soviet citizens who died in 1941–5. But alas for our conception of World War II we still forget all those Chinese slaughtered between 1937–45, a much longer time-frame.

The Eurocentric view of war held by many countries ignores all the fighting that took place in East Asia before 1941, when Japan invaded the colonial properties of Britain, the USA, France and the Netherlands. Even before Pearl Harbor in December 1941, the European allies were drawn into the Asian conflict to protect their colonial investments.

While the Pacific war is certainly not forgotten in the USA, America in 1941 was joining in a struggle that was already years

---

WHEN DID WORLD WAR II BEGIN?

Consider these dates:
   1 September 1939: Germany invades Poland
   3 September 1939: Britain and France declare war on Germany
   22 June 1941: Germany invades the USSR
   7 December 1941: Japan attacks the US fleet in Pearl Harbor
All these are legitimate dates for the start of World War II. But a different view, propounded by Evan Mawdsley in *World War II: A New History* fulfils the title's promise and comes up with a new date: 7 July 1937. The 'Marco Polo Bridge Incident' was the start of the real war between China and Japan that continued right through until the Japanese surrender in August 1945.

If our conflict really is a world war, this non-Eurocentric date makes a lot of sense – even if the war in Europe took another two years to begin, and the USA and the USSR, the two main victorious allies, another four to enter. If British historians can begin the fighting in 1939, two years prior to Pearl Harbor and to *Barbarossa*, why can't we start the war in 1937, when Japan invaded the main part of China?

old. Pearl Harbor was the date on which the USA entered an existing fight.

China and the background to war

After the fall of the Manchu dynasty in 1912, China was in theory ruled by the Guomindang, the followers of the great revolutionary hero Sun Yat-sen. But in practice much of the territory of the country was dominated by semi-independent warlords, who made their own decisions and usually ignored those of the notionally Nationalist government based in Nanking, under the Guomindang leader Chiang Kai-shek.

Just to make life more difficult for the Nationalists, much of China was also Communist controlled, under the man who would, after his victory in 1949, become world famous: Mao Zedong. One of the Nationalist leader Chiang's greatest problems was always: whom should he fight? Mao or the Japanese? Could he afford to fight both? And the same dilemma sometimes occurred to Mao, since he was not always as active in fighting the Japanese during this period as he later wanted history to think.

But in 1937, Chiang's feelings and options were clear. Manchuria – the original homeland of the Manchu (or Ching) dynasty – had been ruled by the Japanese since 1931. Japan had not been actively involved in trying to conquer any part of original ethnic Chinese territory. With the attack at Beijing, things had changed and active resistance had become necessary.

Many countries – Britain and the USA included– had extraterritorial settlements in parts of China. Some of these, like Hong Kong, dated back to times of Chinese weakness in the nineteenth century. Shanghai was international territory, where the writ of the Chinese government did not apply. One of these Shanghai extra-territorial areas was occupied by Japan, which entitled the Japanese to station troops there. Chiang took the bold decision to attack the Japanese-controlled area of the city. As many

Europeans lived in concession areas under foreign rule, everyone became involved in the fight that ensued.

1937 and the beginning of the war

Unfortunately the Nationalist troops were no match for the Japanese forces, which included the latter's navy, as Shanghai was accessible by sea. By November, the Chinese were forced into an ignominious withdrawal. As a result, the Japanese were able to launch a devastating counter-attack. They seized the former Nationalist capital of Nanking, massacring thousands of innocent civilians in the process, one of the worst war crimes of the whole conflict.

THE RAPE OF NANKING

When we think of major atrocities committed during World War II it is usually the Holocaust and the murder of six million Jews to which we turn. But as the surviving British prisoners of war of the Japanese remind us, the Japanese were equally bestial in their treatment of innocent civilians. The Japanese believed themselves to be a divine race, and that the Chinese were below the level of pigs.

All in all some twenty million Chinese died between 1937 and 1945, a figure that dwarfs most of the losses from Europe. When the Japanese attacked the city of Nanking in December they slaughtered somewhere between 200,000 and 300,000 innocent people, tens of thousands of whom were women who were raped first and then murdered, usually brutally. In what is known as the Rape of Nanking or in modern terminology the Nanjing Massacre, Chinese soldiers who had surrendered were beheaded wholesale.

A German eyewitness, John Rabe, put it:

I am totally puzzled by the conduct of the Japanese. On the one hand, they want to be recognized and treated as a great power on a par with the European powers, on the other, they are currently displaying a crudity, brutality and bestiality that bears no comparison except with the hordes of Genghis Khan.

As the Japanese began, so they were to continue throughout the war. The treatment of conquered women exceeds anything that the Nazis perpetrated. While the Japanese did not have an official policy of genocide, such as that of the Third Reich, in practice there is no real difference between the barbarities inflicted by the two countries during the war. It is hardly surprising that China remains wary of Japan to this day.

The world now had to take notice – this was not a localised spat. In the USA, millions of Americans had close emotional ties to China through the international Christian movements that had begun in the nineteenth century, with thousands of Americans serving in the region over decades. (And non-Americans served too, such as the Scottish Olympic athlete Eric Liddell, immortalised in the film *Chariots of Fire*). Trade, too, played a part, especially in the great treaty ports such as Shanghai. In October 1937, US president Franklin Roosevelt called for a quarantine against all aggressor states. However, nothing much was done to follow up, and the only aid that came to the stricken Nationalists was from the USSR, which sent 1,600 aircraft and some 5,000 or so 'advisers' to lend a hand. (Stalin was never sure in this period whether to support Chiang or Mao. His decisive switch to his fellow Communists came after 1945.)

The war soon became a bloodbath. Many of these deaths occurred during some particularly savage fighting in June 1938, when the Nationalists, in sheer desperation at Japanese successes, decided to breach the Yellow River dykes. This had the desired effect of slowing the Japanese juggernaut. However, it resulted, it has been estimated, in floods that caused the deaths of countless innocent Chinese civilians lower down the river. Thus,

Nationalist victory was gained at considerable expense to their own population.

The Chinese army, Soviet aid notwithstanding, was not the best equipped. There was also endemic corruption, and the fact that many warlords were fighting as much for themselves as for their supposed country. This in turn, it has been argued, provided the Japanese army with less incentive to modernise, with militarily catastrophic effects when it came to taking on the far more updated American and Australian forces, especially after the turning of the Pacific War in favour of the Allies. The expense of waging war on so colossal a front was overwhelming and, after the attack on Pearl Harbor in December 1941, it was to prove fatal for the Imperial government. Fighting all over China with their army and across the Pacific with their navy, a two-front war, was well above any available Japanese resources.

The Japanese in 1937–8 aimed for what they called *Sokk-sen, sokk-katsu*. This was a Japanese version of blitzkrieg although its translation ('quick war, quick settlement') was nineteenth-century Prussian in origin. Whatever it was, it failed totally. However far the Japanese went, the Nationalists could retreat, and still be in Chinese-controlled territory. Over a million Japanese troops were fighting in different parts of the country.

In the north in 1940, for instance, there was the 'Hundred Regiments Offensive' between about 400,000 Communist-controlled troops and the Japanese. This slowed the former, but without clear victory – and by 1941 Nationalists and Communists were fighting each other again and not the Japanese. Similar battles were waged in the south, but again with no real knockout blow landed by the invaders against their Chinese enemies. No matter how hard the Japanese attacked there was always somewhere for their opponents to go.

Overall, Japan lost approximately 220,000 troops between 1937–9 and a further 100,000 in 1940–1, with perhaps as many as 1,030,000 Chinese deaths altogether. This meant that from

1937–41, before the Japanese took on the USA, Japan had already lost as many troops as the USA would suffer on all fronts in the entire war from 1941–5.

The battle that helped to determine World War II

We tend to separate the war in Europe from that in Asia. But in August to September 1939, a battle took place near a remote part of East Asia that made all the difference to the war in Europe and, as we now see, could well have altered the outcome of the entire war, in both Europe and Asia at the same time.

What was it that made this confrontation, with tension that had started in May 1939, pivotal both for World War II and for the Allies?

In August 1939, Soviet and Japanese armies vied with each other in Khalkin Gol, a region on the Mongolian/Chinese (Manchurian) border, sometimes also known as Nomonhan. In this crucially significant battle the Red Army commander was none other than Georgii Zhukov, who later went on to be the most successful Allied military leader of World War II.

Some 10,000 Soviet troops were killed, and no fewer than 25,000 Japanese. By the later standards of carnage, these figures are low. But they were to have a major impact on the rest of the war. This seemingly insignificant battle was to change the position of the USSR in the war and led to Japanese aggression against the USA. Soviet victory caused Japan to take the 'southern option' and to invade the European-ruled territories of Southeast Asia and the Pacific – and not west, towards Siberia. Going south would lead to war with the USA, to Pearl Harbor and to ultimate Japanese defeat in 1945.

With hindsight, we take Japan's decision to go south for granted. But it also completely changed the war in Europe. With the Japanese decision to remain neutral in relation to the USSR – to reject an invasion of Siberia – and the Soviet Union reciprocating until after V-E Day in 1945, Stalin only had to worry about a war on his European Front. In December 1941, the Soviets came within a hairsbreadth of losing Moscow and possibly therefore the war. But because in April 1941 Japan and the USSR had signed a treaty of neutrality, Stalin could send Red Army troops from the eastern parts of the country to defend European Russia against the Germans. This helped tip the balance on the Eastern Front, enabling the Soviets to survive and then to be on the winning side in 1945.

Had the Soviets had to fight a two-front war, in both Europe and the Far East, against both the Japanese and the Germans, they would certainly have lost. Possibly World War II would have taken infinitely longer to win (with America in the war from December 1941 to make victory possible). Or perhaps the Axis defeat of the USSR would have so altered its course in their favour that Hitler and his Japanese partner would have won instead.

In which case history would have been very different…

But with Zhukov's decisive battle over the Kwantung army at Khalkin Gol, the Japanese decided to go south, not west. Stalin's USSR was safe until Hitler invaded it in June 1941, and the Allies went on to win.

So Khalkin Gol determined the key strategic outcomes of the conflict: the need for the Soviets to fight the war on one front only until the defeat of Germany, and the Japanese decision to attack the USA.

In the last chapter, we saw that the Molotov–Ribbentrop Pact entirely changed the nature of the war, since Hitler no longer had to worry about war with the USSR. He could invade Poland in conjunction with Stalin and then, when ready, turn westwards. And Stalin, with no Japanese threat to worry him thanks to Khalkin Gol, could simply watch his capitalist enemies fighting it out between them.

The war in Asia and the links to the rest of the world

In September 1939, Europe joined in a conflagration that had already erupted two years earlier in East Asia. And Britain, in doing so, began in what in reality was a massively disadvantageous position. By December 1941, and the Japanese attacks on Britain's imperial possessions in East Asia, all the very worst possible nightmares of the British chiefs of staff (the professional heads of the army, Royal Air Force and Royal Navy) had come all too horribly true. Britain was simultaneously at war with Germany, Italy and Japan, the very situation that the armed services had spent the 1930s trying all they could to avoid. There was absolutely no way in which Britain could win such a war unaided, and in June 1940 the only reliable continental ally, France, had been humiliatingly defeated.

The issue, therefore, boils down to this: if the chiefs of staff were right, does this make appeasement and the policy of the Baldwin and Chamberlain governments correct? Or was Churchill right to say that there was a very real alternative and that if decisions had been different Britain would still have been at war with Germany – and eventually Japan, but maybe not Italy – and in a far stronger position with which to wage what was an inevitable war?

Some months later, in April 1941, the Japanese and Soviets signed a neutrality agreement. This meant that each country only had to fight on one front: Japan in their invasion south into Asia and the Soviets on their western border with Europe. And Stalin was hoping to postpone war, either against Japan or against Germany, for as long as possible.

The Nazi–Soviet Pact, often called the Molotov–Ribbentrop Pact after the two foreign ministers who signed it (Vyacheslav Molotov for the USSR, Joachim Ribbentrop for Hitler), was the game changer that made the critical difference as to how World War

II was fought. The two major dictatorships in Europe, the Soviet Union and the Third Reich, agreed not to go to war. This meant that for all intents and purposes Hitler and Stalin were friendly non-belligerents, with the USSR agreeing to give major supplies – notably oil – to Germany. Hitler did not need to fear a two-front war (the German mistake of World War I) and Stalin, who had so recently purged much of his army's leadership, no longer feared invasion. The capitalist powers could fight it out while he waited peacefully in the wings.

The Japanese Imperial government was so shocked at the news of the Nazi–Soviet Pact that it resigned. They had for years regarded the USSR as a major potential or actual enemy, and so the signature of a pact with the Soviets by Japan's supposed friend Nazi Germany was seen, as it indeed was, as a great betrayal of trust and friendship. In so resigning, the Japanese leadership set in motion a chain of events that completely altered the outcome of the war that they had started in China in 1937 and which soon now became truly global – World War II. For the war in East Asia, we will need another chapter.

HIRANUMA KIICHIRŌ

Hiranuma Kiichirō is not a familiar name in the West, even though convicted of being a Class A war criminal in 1945 by the victorious Allies. He was prime minister of Japan from January 1939 to 30 August 1939.

What is significant is his resignation date. The Japanese had not been consulted about the Molotov–Ribbentrop Pact, and were speechless that their supposed friend, Germany, had signed a non-aggression treaty with what the Japanese thought was their mutual Communist enemy, the USSR. The Nazi–Soviet Pact threw the Japanese into a spin, and the Hiranuma government resigned – though it should be added that the defeat by Soviet troops at Khalkin Gol also added to the sense of disaster.

Bloodlands: the carnage of the lands between Germany and Russia

From the viewpoint of both Stalin and Hitler, the key clauses of the Nazi–Soviet Pact of August 1939 were the secret annexes that carved up Central Europe between them – what Yale historian Timothy Snyder accurately calls in his book '*Bloodlands*'. Poland was divided into two, so that Stalin was able to acquire the territory the USSR had wanted but lost between 1919–21. Hitler would now find it much easier to invade Poland, since the Poles would be facing a Soviet invasion from the east as well as the German attack from the west. The three Baltic states of Latvia, Lithuania and Estonia, which had escaped the Russian Empire in 1917–18, would now once more be under Moscow's control (and in 1940 the USSR annexed them).

For a long time, the aims and policies of the USSR under Stalin were a mystery. Thanks now to historians such as Gabriel Gorodetsky, John Lewis Gaddis and Jonathan Haslam who were able to delve in the archives when Gorbachev's *glasnost* policy declassified them in the 1980s, we have an accurate picture of what was going on within the Soviet government and Politburo. Those such as Litvinov, who wanted an anti-fascist front were sidelined, and hard-nosed people such as Molotov prevailed in the internal debates, putting the safety of the USSR above the ideological differences between Nazism and Communism.

Initially, the Pact (and the follow-up agreement a month later) massively benefited the Germans, who were now able to conquer the rest of Europe with impunity. Ultimately, it sealed the Third Reich's doom, since it prevented the war against the Soviets that many Japanese wanted. As we saw, the Soviets only had to fight Hitler. When the Wehrmacht was at the gates of Moscow in December 1941 this was to make the critical difference between defeat and survival.

Poland betrayed: invaded from east and from west

The fall of Poland was now only a matter of time. With enemies on both sides, the Poles succumbed bravely but quickly. Germany invaded on 1 September 1939 – the day World War II in Europe truly began. Since Hitler refused to withdraw, Britain and France declared war on the Third Reich on 3 September, the day most European schoolchildren are taught as the date World War II commenced.

Hitherto, history has concentrated on the Nazi atrocities only. The bombing of so many civilians in Warsaw presaged the slaughter of millions of civilians in the next six years, and the SS began its task not just of exterminating Jews but also eliminating as much of the leadership of Poland as possible. *Lebensraum* involved the displacement or death of countless Gentile Poles as well as Jewish, since the Slavic races were as *untermenschen* or subhuman as the Semitic.

What is often forgotten, because of *Operation Barbarossa* and the USSR being on our side after June 1941, is that the atrocities committed on the German part of the new divide were replicated in full on the Soviet section of Poland as well. Jews were not targeted as such, but since many of them were prosperous they,

THE KATYN MASSACRE

On 5 March 1940, Stalin and Beria, the head of the NKVD, the Soviet secret police, authorised through the Politburo that thousands of Polish officers and other leading officials should be shot. Some 21,892 of them were rounded up and murdered in various forests in western Russia. The biggest single death toll was in the Katyn Forest, though since the exact number executed is a source of often vituperative disagreement between the Poles and the Russians to this day, we cannot know for certain how many thousands died at that actual site.

The slaughter was, unfortunately, discovered in 1943 and by the Nazis, which meant that Stalin was able to dismiss it as German propaganda. Many in Britain knew that the discovery was genuine, but it was not until the 1970s that agitation began to get the real perpetrators accused of war crimes. Poland was itself under Communist rule until 1989, and so it was 1990 before the Soviet leader Mikhail Gorbachev confessed that the NKVD was the guilty party and that the truth had been hidden for decades.

As we are now realising, the massacre was only one of the atrocities that the Soviets committed against the Poles. Laurence Rees' book and television documentary *World War II: Behind Closed Doors* has shown to a shocked new generation the true horrors of the USSR's crimes against Poland between 1939–41 and again in 1944–5 when the Red Army invaded former Polish territory to reach Germany.

along with thousands of other members of the pre-war Polish elite were singled out either for death or for transportation, in the latter case to places hundreds of miles away in what is now the Russian Far East or to Kazakhstan. Race was the motivation for the Nazis, class for the Soviets, but the actual effect was precisely the same: hundreds of thousands were slaughtered, transported or herded like cattle into prisons and what would be, in the USSR as well as the Third Reich, death camps, the NKVD being as fully-practiced in mass murder as the SS.

The phony war: fighting Hitler from the periphery

As Mawdsley puts it, Britain and France now embarked on a strategy 'that with hindsight [seems] incomprehensible and even ridiculous'. If anything this is an understatement, since the 'peripheral strategy' doctrine was believed in as much by Winston Churchill throughout the conflict as by the disastrous Neville Chamberlain and French leader Edouard Daladier in

1939–40. Rather than attack Germany direct – on land or by air – they decided on building up alliances on the edges of German-controlled territory, principally in the Balkans but also, if possible, in Scandinavia as well.

At one stage, the Allies even thought of going to war with the USSR to protect Finland, a neutral country that the Soviets invaded, but which the Red Army was not able fully to conquer. There were also plans to bomb the Baku oil fields in the Caucasus, in order to prevent Soviet oil from reaching Germany under the Nazi–Soviet Pact. The Turks were able to stop this folly from occurring, since the best route for Allied bombers was over Turkish soil, and that government refused overflight rights.

Then in April 1940, Hitler began his invasion of Western Europe, and the day of reckoning that Britain and France had for so long sought to postpone truly came at last.

3

The Hinge of War: Britain Surviving May 1940–December 1941

Historians love the word 'hinge': a crucial happening upon which great events turn. Churchill called volume 4 of his epic history of World War II, *The Hinge of Fate*, covering in this instance the years 1942–3. Many would agree with such a diagnosis, even if we would now give more relative importance to the siege of Stalingrad (1942–3) than to the Battle of Alamein in late 1942. It was during that period, most argue, that the war turned decisively in favour of the Allies, and an Axis victory became impossible.

There is very considerable truth in such a thesis, and much sense in saying that that was indeed when the Axis effectively lost the war, even though the conflict continued another bloodthirsty two years until 1945.

However, there is another equally vital hinge period, the one that we are covering in this chapter: May 1940 to December 1941.

Britain and its Empire alone against the foe

In May 1940, Churchill became prime minister of the United Kingdom and de facto leader of the British Empire, since India, Canada, Australia and New Zealand all played a very active role defending Britain against the Axis. In December 1941, the

WINSTON CHURCHILL

Winston Churchill (1874–1965) was voted the Greatest Briton in a BBC poll following a series in November 2002. Even if the seventeenth-century leader Oliver Cromwell has a strong claim to such a title (as argued by his supporters during the BBC series), he is certainly the most famous and revered of recent centuries. While revisionists, from American mavericks to serious historians, have tried to topple him from his perch, the more we know about the 1930s and 1940s, the more secure is his reputation as the person who did rescue Britain in 1940–41.

Yet as Robert Rhodes James rightly points out in his book *Winston Churchill: A Study in Failure 1900–1939*, had he died in, say, 1938, he would be regarded as a great man but certainly not the superhero which we perceive him to be today. Until May 1940 when he became prime minister (and, equally crucially, minister of defence), he had a distinctly erratic reputation. He changed political allegiance not once, but twice, and was responsible for some catastrophic misjudgements in World War I such as the Allied defeat in the Dardanelles fiasco in 1915–16. His bold but overambitious idea of capturing the capital of the Ottoman Empire failed, thus leading to one of the major and most unnecessary defeats of that conflict. It is true that from 1933 he resolutely opposed Hitler and attacked appeasement, but he was out of office not so much for that as for his equally implacable opposition to Indian independence, a quixotic stand that made him look antediluvian as well as erratic.

All this meant, though, that when he finally achieved office as First Lord of the Admiralty in September 1939 he was seen as untainted by the policies of the appeasers. His old-fashioned imperialism became a virtue as he defended Britain and its empire against the horrors of Nazism and, as American journalist Ed Murrow put it, he 'gave the British lion its roar' in the sheer power of his oratory and inspiring leadership.

Churchill's interference in strategy – he would micromanage even down to battalion level and was forever changing generals – infuriated his commanders and professional advisers. This policy of the 'indirect approach', attacking Germany through the 'underbelly' of Italy, drove the Americans to distraction. But he always understood the big picture and never completely overrode the generals, especially Sir Alan Brooke, his chief of the imperial general staff. And, in any case, after 1943, the ultimate decisions were out of his hands, whatever his protests, as the USA took the lead in strategy.

For increasingly Churchill the patriot came to realise that Britain was no longer the major world player that it had been most of his long life. Critics have attacked him for what they perceive as giving away his country's standing – as if the British Empire could have lasted indefinitely through the kind of deal with Hitler in 1940 that he rejected as unthinkable and would surely have been immoral. Britain was bankrupt by the end of the war and the USA the undoubted superpower – but could it have been otherwise?

Writers such as Max Hastings have suggested that perhaps his greatest achievement was to see – almost uniquely among the British politicians of his time – that only through American entry into the war could Britain survive. In this he was to prove triumphantly correct, and in keeping the United Kingdom and its empire in the war without being conquered by Hitler from May 1940 to December 1941, when the USA joined the conflict, he succeeded when all else seemed lost. The fact that Britain was on the winning side is entirely thanks to him. Since the USA could never have launched the re-conquest of Europe had Churchill lost, the very survival of democracy owes him everything. For once, the hyperbole really is the truth.

Japanese made the catastrophic strategic error of attacking the United States. That decision, along with Hitler's equally foolish declaration of war on the USA, brought America into the war and changed its outcome in favour of the Allies.

Furthermore, two key things happened during that time: Britain survived on its own in Europe, and Hitler invaded the USSR, but failed to capture it, showing that blitzkrieg no longer worked.

In other words, the survival of Germany's two key enemies – the UK and the Soviet Union – ensured that when the USA entered the war after Pearl Harbor, the American policy of defeating Germany first could be implemented successfully, and that the outcome of the war, and the defeat of the Axis, was sooner or later inevitable. Without Britain as its aircraft carrier to liberate Europe, the defeat of Nazi Germany would have taken the

Americans inexorably longer. If the Soviets had been defeated, the Axis could have linked up and the defeat of Japan would have been significantly harder to achieve.

All the pieces of the jigsaw need to be considered if one is to understand the war properly, which means linking what happened in Europe to events in Asia, and taking the fate of the USSR very seriously. All this is central to an understanding of the conflict of 1937–45.

This approach might seem to marginalise Britain. But the stubborn resistance of the British Empire forced Hitler to fight on two fronts after June 1941, with repercussions for the Eastern Front. His obsession with Britain was a reason behind Barbarossa, since to his thinking the defeat of the USSR would force the

CHURCHILL'S SPEECHES AND THE GREAT REPUBLIC

Churchill's oratory helped the British people to keep going in the dark days of 1940–1, the generation that survived the Blitz. Even today, people alive at that time still get goose bumps listening to those words or, in the case of one survivor, being shown the actual notes Churchill used to make one of his speeches.

An interesting codicil – only MPs heard the originals, since there was no broadcasting from the House of Commons. The speeches were rerecorded and rebroadcast, and it was to those which people sat around their radio sets during the war to listen.

Churchill did not just have a domestic audience but an equally vital, if not actually more important, transatlantic one as well: the people and government of the USA. Look at some familiar speeches from 1940 and then consider the highlighted parts – it is clear that his intended listeners were as much in Washington, DC as in the bomb-struck cities of Britain.

First, we can consider his *We Shall Fight Them on the Beaches* speech of 4 June. The famous part is perhaps not the most important:

> We shall go on to the end. We shall fight in France, we shall fight on the seas and oceans, we shall fight with growing confidence and growing strength in the air, we shall

> defend our island, whatever the cost may be. We shall fight
> on the beaches, we shall fight on the landing grounds, we
> shall fight in the fields and in the streets, we shall fight in
> the hills; we shall never surrender, and if, which I do not
> for a moment believe, this island or a large part of it were
> subjugated and starving, then our Empire beyond the seas,
> armed and guarded by the British Fleet, would carry on the
> struggle, until, in God's good time, the New World, with
> all its power and might, steps forth to the rescue and the
> liberation of the old.

Britain would fight on to the very end – there would be no shabby compromise peace of the kind that Pétain had made. But notice the plea: 'until, in God's good time, the New World...' Canada was already at war, so this is evidently directed at the USA, the one country, as Churchill knew well, that could defeat the Nazis and rescue Britain and the world from the Nazi threat. Britain's old policy, of relying on a continental ally, was no longer possible, but now America, if engaged, could enter the fray and alter the outcome.

Second, here is an extract from the *Finest Hour* speech, on 18 June, with the Battle of Britain beginning:

> Upon this battle depends the survival of Christian civiliza-
> tion...our own British life... [Britain would resist Hitler.]
> But if we fail, then the whole world, including the United
> States, including all that we have known and cared for, will
> sink into the abyss of a new Dark Age made more sinister,
> and perhaps more protracted, by the lights of perverted
> science.

In other words, it was more than just British survival but the very essence of civilised society, of democratic values and freedoms that was at stake, a message that would resonate in American ears. And if Britain fell, then the USA would be affected too, especially since it was not just Germany that would have prevailed, but Nazism, something altogether more sinister and vile.

Churchill knew of course how hamstrung Roosevelt was in June 1940, both by the need to get re-elected that November and by the USA's draconian Neutrality Acts. But unlike most other British politicians, he also understood that it was only US entry into the war that could rescue Britain from sure defeat.

British to make peace, something Churchill was always refusing to contemplate.

Churchill's resilience, and that of the generation that survived the Blitz, had an enormous psychological impact on the USA, and in particular on those who wanted America to play its part in the struggle for democracy. His speeches deliberately encouraged not only the besieged Britons listening to them in bomb shelters, but thousands of both ordinary and influential Americans who heard them thousands of miles away across the Atlantic. Nazi victory was not inevitable, and American participation could still make a difference. The isolationist case surely diminished every day that Britain, and later also the USSR, survived the worst that the Nazis could do.

So while what follows from May 1940 to December 1941 is not at the heart of the conflict that would erupt once the USA entered and the Japanese took the war beyond China into the wider Pacific, nonetheless it made what happened next possible.

The fall of France and its consequences

While we know now that the Axis was eventually defeated, things did not look at all bright in May 1940, when Winston Churchill took office. Within days, the Netherlands, a country neutral in World War I, surrendered and not long after Belgium, whose security was vital to both France and Britain, followed, with King Leopold earning much ignominy for refusing to flee the country. King Haakon VII of Norway, by contrast, fled to Britain on 9 June, an icon for his nation's resistance to Nazi occupation.

British military planners euphemistically called the collapse of France 'a certain eventuality' and within a week of Churchill becoming prime minister that scenario became a virtual certainty. Reynaud, the beleaguered French leader, increasingly gave way to the defeatists, and on 18 May made the blunder of putting Marshal Pétain, the hero of World War I, into his Cabinet. Pétain was no hero this time around and the chaos in France worsened exponentially. French generals began weeping uncontrollably rather than inspiring their troops.

The strategic genius of General Erich von Manstein's 'sickle cut' or *Sichelsnitt* plan, was to drive a wedge between Anglo-French forces on the Belgian border and the other part of the French army to the south. In particular, panzer general Heinz Guderian and another future star, Erwin Rommel, created their daring reputations by sweeping their tanks across the River Meuse and cutting the Allied forces off from one another. Soon they were at the Channel, a dash of over 150 miles in just under a week that was virtually unparalleled in military history.

The fall of France to Germany in June 1940 remains one of the biggest mysteries in the history of warfare. It has rightly been called the *Strange Victory*, since militarily the odds were heavily stacked on the French side and not the German.

By all possible measures of calculation, the French army outclassed the Wehrmacht in every one. Even their tanks were superior to those of Germany, and the size of the Allied armies combined easily outweighed that of the invaders.

In the past, people puzzled how a nation as mighty as France could fall, and decided that the answer to the mystery was that the French were a nation of cowards with decadence rife. The country had shrunk behind the imaginary invincibility of the Maginot Line, the great chain of fortresses designed to protect the country against the successful German invasion of 1870 and the near miss of 1914. France, with hatred between political right and left, especially after the victory of the Popular Front in 1936, was a nation divided against itself.

Most historians now reject this, and instead put the reason – still hotly contested – down to two factors:

1 The mainly defensive strategy of the French military leadership.
2 The brilliant opportunism and strategic good luck of the Germans.

This explanation makes more sense, since previous attempts are really excuses for French failure often made by those with domestic political axes to grind, on both sides of the spectrum.

The German strategic genius showed that blitzkrieg worked – at least in countries with proper roads. The British troops were now effectively isolated and evacuation was the only possibility. It is sometimes said that it is better to be a general on the winning side at the end of a war rather than at the beginning. This was certainly true of the British Expeditionary Force commander Lord Gort. He had no option but to evacuate his forces, starting on 26 May, from the port of Dunkirk. The good news was that 340,000 soldiers (one-third French, many of whom opted to return to their country, and two-thirds British) were successfully taken off the beaches, the bad news being that they had to leave nearly all their equipment behind. While the Royal Navy rescued most of the soldiers, large numbers were also ferried across the English Channel in small boats, by doughty fishermen and other civilians who risked their lives to save the troops.

Arguably, the evacuation was only able to take place because the Germans had decided on 24 May to halt their panzer divisions for a refit. This action proved enormously controversial after the war, as Wehrmacht leaders blamed Hitler for the British escape. Dunkirk itself, while a terrible defeat for Britain, has gone down in legend as a 'miracle' because so many were evacuated, many in those famous 'little ships' which took the troops off the beaches and into the safe hands of the Royal Navy. But while many rejoiced at the return of the British Expeditionary Force (BEF) back home, Churchill was very aware of the true magnitude of the defeat.

France did not last much longer. On 16 June, Pétain became prime minister, and the next day he began negotiations with Germany. On 22 June, Hitler forced the French to sign an armistice in the same railway carriage in which the Germans had surrendered in 1918. There was to be no legal French government in exile, unlike many other European countries whose political leaders had fled. The northern part of France, including Paris, was to be under direct German control. In the south, a puppet French government was established under Pétain, at the spa town of Vichy, which gave its name to the new regime.

Not all French people agreed with this calumny, however. A junior general managed to escape to London to continue the resistance with British backing. His name would become legendary: Charles de Gaulle.

Britain's survival and the 'pivotal moment'

For Britain the fall of France was what David Reynolds has rightly called a pivotal moment. Since Churchill's famous ancestor, the great John Churchill, first Duke of Marlborough, defeated the French at victories such as Blenheim, the British had always relied on continental armies to win land-based wars for them, and on the global reach and power of the Royal Navy to do the rest.

While past British soldiers fought on European soil – notably under Wellington – they could not have won without large numbers of foreign troops under their command as well, while illustrious admirals such as Nelson won the critical battles at sea. Not until the first few months of World War I did what historians call the continental commitment change in nature. The stalemate of the Western Front in Flanders obliged the British to place a gigantic, continental-size army on European soil.

We now tend to think of large British conscript armies, of the kind seen in both world wars, as being the usual pattern. This is far from the case historically, since the nation's leaders saw World War I as an aberration, not the norm.

As a result, the fall of France saw Britain without a major European ally and with no military means of getting back to

the Continent to continue the fight against Hitler. This created
an unprecedented situation, as there was no continental ally to
provide the large conscript army necessary to win a war. Churchill realised this. His first response was to continue to fight. His
second response was to attempt to win for the Allied cause the
power of the United States, a country which, while not a continental European power, possessed the potential resources well
above any of Britain's previous land-based Allies.

Britain's centuries-old strategy, the peripheral approach, was
to attack the enemy sideways rather than straight on. Historically, this involved using Britannia's domination of the waves to
win at sea. Since this was dependent upon the Royal Navy, a
large conscript army had been unnecessary. Part of this traditional strategy entailed blockading the enemy. War was waged
through economic means while the land-based Allies fought on
continental soil, albeit often under a British commander, such as
the Dukes of Marlborough or of Wellington. But now no such
land-based ally existed.

Churchill and the great republic: the leader who understood the USA

Churchill now took some major decisions. On the one hand,
he realised – virtually alone among the British political/military
elite – that the USA was the answer. For Chamberlain, America
represented 'nothing but words', for Churchill, the USA was the
great republic, the arsenal of democracy.

Today, we take the USA as a superpower for granted. In 1940,
it was still steeped in isolation, its appearance as a global power
from 1917–19 very much more the exception than the norm.
Roosevelt was secretly profoundly sympathetic to the British
struggle against Nazism – awkwardly for Churchill, he was also a
zealous anti-imperialist who rejected the latter's belief in empire.
Outwardly, at least until the November 1940 presidential elections
were over, Roosevelt espoused a cautious official neutrality.

FRANKLIN ROOSEVELT

Franklin Delano Roosevelt (FDR: 1882–1945) was, like Winston Churchill, an aristocrat in politics, but in his case a political liberal from a republic, the USA. He was elected president for a unique four terms from 1933–45. He won in 1940 – to the relief of the British, and once re-elected aimed to ensure that America would do everything possible to guarantee the defeat of the dictatorships.

Roosevelt's first two terms were mainly centred on domestic themes, such as the new deal, which was aimed at enabling the USA to recover from the great depression. He also had to cope with a strongly isolationist Congress and an American people who were sceptical about the merits of the USA's involvement in a European war in 1917–18. Thankfully, his talented chief of army staff General George C. Marshall understood the need even in peacetime to increase the size of the armed forces (America's army in 1939 was no bigger than Belgium's). So when it came to Britain, Roosevelt was able to give that beleaguered country all 'help short of war' in terms of war material and support.

In 1941, on 7 December, the 'day that shall live in infamy' according to Roosevelt, Japan attacked the USA in Pearl Harbor. America was finally in the conflict. Hitler's decision to declare war on the USA enabled Roosevelt, Marshall and other leaders who favoured the 'Germany First' policy to concentrate on the war against the Third Reich. Here was a different policy from that of the US Navy and millions of Americans who wanted to give the priority to revenge on Japan. This turned out greatly to Britain's advantage; though as Churchill was to discover, the sheer industrial and military might of the now superpower USA was soon to make that country far more important in the war effort than the fragile United Kingdom and its empire.

Always an idealist in the mould of Woodrow Wilson, but a far more astute politician, Roosevelt felt that he could change the world order for the better. This sometimes entailed being nicer to Stalin than to Churchill, to the latter's sorrow. Roosevelt believed that without the co-operation of the USSR the defeat of Japan would take longer. Furthermore, the new United Nations structure – a force for peace much stronger than the failed League of Nations – needed full Soviet collaboration to work.

FDR can be said to be the first American president of the kind of America we know today – the leader of the free world. Whatever his flaws, he was able to lead his country to victory both in Europe and in Asia, dying just weeks before V-E Day and the culmination of all his efforts.

Churchill's flagrant wooing of the USA has come under fire by revisionist historians; so too has his other key decision, taken in May 1940, and deliberately underplayed in his memoirs, which was to refuse all negotiations with Hitler. This took some persuading of sceptical colleagues, but thankfully for him his predecessor Neville Chamberlain weighed in behind him and any talk of opening discussions via Mussolini was overwhelmingly defeated. Had Britain surrendered in 1940, it does not bear thinking how terrible the consequences would have been, including for any American long-term plan for rescuing Europe from dictatorship.

Britain: alone in Europe but far from alone

One should add that Churchill equally understood the vital contribution that the empire could make – Canada, Australia and New Zealand all played a key role in the conflict, in both North Africa and in Europe, especially after the landings in Normandy on D-Day in 1944. The many thousands of Polish soldiers and airmen who escaped the Nazi–Soviet invasion were equally critical in Allied success. The myth that Britain stood 'alone' in 1940 makes wonderful jingoistic propaganda, but it is entirely untrue and slanders the countless intrepid Poles and Commonwealth forces that came to the rescue.

In 1940, the United Kingdom nearly fell too. But the Royal Navy and the pilots of the RAF prevailed. The excellent TV series *Foyle's War*, broadcast in both the UK and the USA, conveys an accurate impression of England at that time. The sense of fear pervading Britain was understandably powerful. London would have been swiftly captured. But the Luftwaffe failed, and Hitler cancelled *Sealion*, his planned invasion of Britain.

Roosevelt and the millions of Americans who supported Britain and the cause of democracy were greatly relieved at the narrow survival of the United Kingdom. On the one hand, isolationist

THE BATTLE OF BRITAIN

The Battle of Britain and the narrow victory of the Royal Air Force over the invading German Luftwaffe made a pivotal difference to Allied victory in World War II. Not merely a single battle, the Battle of Britain began with what Hitler deemed to be Eagle Day on 13 August 1940. It lasted until his decision to postpone – but in reality to cancel – *Sealion* on 17 September. This latter operation would have been the land and sea invasion of Britain due for the autumn. The aerial battles between fighter pilots over southeast England enabled the British Isles to survive and fight another day.

Not surprisingly, Churchill, the great orator, likened the brave pilots – many of whom were Polish or Canadian as well as British – to 'the few'. Here his reference is to the heroic soldiers in medieval France under Henry V as interpreted by Shakespeare. And certainly, the sheer survival at all of the RAF, heavily denuded of resources before 1939, was remarkable, even if victory was by a hairsbreadth.

However, it should be added that while the RAF won, making up for the ignominious failure of the army in France, it was the overwhelming power at sea of the Royal Navy, following the apparent defeat in Norway earlier in the year, that made it necessary for Hitler to win air superiority before conquering a virtually defenceless Britain. The soldiers of 'Dad's Army' would, despite their courage, have been no match for a blitzkrieg invasion. The loss of the Battle of Britain meant that Hitler had, in effect, failed to win both sea and air, each one a necessity in invading an island.

Britain therefore survived.

The strategic and political implication of that is the true achievement of the battle. The fact that Churchill was able to keep Britain fighting until the USA entered the war made all the difference to British defeat and victory. The United Kingdom was able to be an unsinkable battleship upon which US troops could land, thereby ensuring that Hitler would have to fight a two-front war: against the British and Americans in the West and Stalin in the East. This alone guaranteed his defeat once he had failed to beat the USSR in 1941 and was only possible because Britain was free and unconquered. Had the Americans not had their British launch base in 1944 or indeed at any other time in the war, D-Day and the fall of Germany would have been infinitely more difficult, if not actually impossible.

All this was due to the sliver of British victory in August to September 1940, as well as to the fact that Britain had, in Churchill, a prime minister for whom surrender was not a viable option. The few saved not just their country but possibly western democracy itself.

opinion in the USA still favoured neutrality. But secretly the US administration began to draw up plans ready for such a time as it became necessary for America to enter the war on Britain's side.

Churchill carried out one much debated act, ordering the Royal Navy to sink the French fleet in Mers-el-Kébir in Algeria, to prevent the Vichy regime handing it over to the Germans. It created much bad blood with France, but it certainly impressed the Americans with evidence of British resolve.

The misnamed 'Blitz' – the name for the bombing of London was taken from the term 'blitzkrieg', which means a fast land-based attack – showed that the great pre-war myth of 'the bomber will always get through' was entirely false. Over 23,000 British civilians died between June and December 1940, including 648 on the infamous raid on Coventry. But the Blitz spirit proved enduring, and British morale did not crack under the weight of bombs. Indeed, if anything it created an atmosphere of defiance, of willingness to defeat Germany and continue the war.

Churchill could not reinvade France. The German strangle-hold was much too powerful. The threat of invasion remained in British eyes, even as Hitler was turning his gaze to the attack on his supposed ally, the USSR.

But Churchill invested in three ways of attack.

Churchill's threefold strategy for survival

The first means of attack was to have bombing raids on Germany. And here one mystery remains – if British morale was unaffected, how did the RAF think that Germany would be any different? We shall look later at the moral issue of mass area bombing by the Allies, but it is odd that one of Bomber Command's arguments was that targeting German civilians would reduce enemy morale, in a way that had not happened in Britain.

The second line of attack was his instruction to 'set Europe ablaze', by mobilising anti-German resistance movements wherever possible. The primary agent for this was the Special Operations Executive (SOE), which parachuted many a daring man or woman into occupied territory. Exciting films have played up the drama: fiction such as *The Guns of Navarone* and *Charlotte Gray* and the true story in Crete told as *Ill Met By Moonlight*. The SOE were mavericks, often quirky, and carried much glamour in their exploits, with the women often being more courageous than the men.

Much ink has been spilled on whether or not special operations were a good idea. In Norway, it helped destroy the Nazi attempts to build an atomic bomb. After 1944 in France, the Resistance was able to achieve much in destroying German infrastructure in a way that greatly aided the invading Allies. But in other nations the brutal Nazi policy of mass retaliation was very costly to innocent civilians, such as in Czechoslovakia or Yugoslavia, where major massacres took place in revenge for German deaths. Perhaps the jury is still out, but it was a way in which Britain could take the war behind enemy lines.

The final option that Churchill took was to increase the stakes in North Africa, which often involved sending vital war material over there that might have been deemed necessary for the defence of Britain's own shores. This war was to last from

ERWIN ROMMEL

Erwin Rommel was one of the most distinguished German commanders during World War II. For his time in northern Africa commanding the Afrika Korps against often poorly led British and British Empire troops, he was given the name the 'desert fox' and was regarded as a military strategist of genius by his opponents.

As often happens, reputations wax and wane. New thinking often tends to the idea that Rommel, while certainly very good, was nowhere near as top class professionally as those German field marshals and generals who commanded armies many times bigger against the Russians on the Eastern Front.

But while he may not have been in charge of millions of troops on Russian soil, his command of a panzer division in France in 1940, where he was extraordinarily successful against the French, should put him near the first division of the Wehrmacht. One of the problems that British generals had was that while they had the decoded German messages broken by the captured Enigma machine, and so knew what Rommel ought to be doing, so great was his dash and sense of originality and boldness that he took wholly unpredictable actions, usually with success. Not until American supplies and, later on, actual US ground forces, came to North Africa was he finally bested.

Furthermore, he was a rare German commander – one with a good human rights record. He was never compromised or besmirched with atrocities, something made easier by never having served on the Eastern Front. He was also increasingly unhappy with Hitler and the direction of the latter's regime, and it is no coincidence that his suicide followed the failure of the July 1944 plot to assassinate Hitler, since his opposition was well known to the Nazi hierarchy. For this almost unique humanity he thus deserves much credit, and perhaps more than those German commanders who were strategically superior to him but whose complicity in Nazi barbarity renders all of them as inhumane.

September 1940 until May 1943, involving British troops – with Australian, New Zealand and Indian forces joining them. Initially, they fought mainly Italian armies and then, after 1941, the German Afrika Korps under their legendary commander, Field Marshal Rommel.

How Franco helped the Allies – by mistake

Britain was fortunate when its enemies made mistakes. One such instance is the vital meeting between the Spanish dictator Francisco

Franco and Adolf Hitler at the town of Hendaye in October 1940, critically just after the German leader had been with his new underlings in Vichy France.

Franco had been deeply indebted to Germany for help in the civil war that raged in Spain from 1936–39. Picasso's celebrated *Guernica* painting is of an air raid on innocent civilians during that struggle. The bombers were from the Luftwaffe and the attack was to prove a foretaste for far more lethal bombing sorties after 1939. But Franco was also greedy for large swathes of the French empire in northern Africa, something that Hitler, with his new deal with Vichy, felt that he could not give.

Not so well known is the fact that Spain also was economically highly dependent on the USA to reconstruct itself after so shattering a civil war. To side with Hitler would cost such American support. And although Franco and much of his cabinet were solidly pro-Axis, this economic factor gave the extraordinarily efficient British diplomatic and spy network in Spain enormous leverage to pressure Spain to stay neutral.

In the end, Gibraltar, a British naval base since the early eighteenth century, remained British and was not seized by Spain, and without Spanish aid a German conquest of Gibraltar would have been difficult to achieve. Franco sent troops to fight the USSR after 1941 but stayed strictly neutral in relation to the Western allies.

This, in turn, meant that Britain could keep the entrance to the Mediterranean open to the Royal Navy and for vital shipping to the considerable British, Indian, Australian and New Zealand armies in North Africa, especially in Egypt. If the Mediterranean had been choked off this would have been considerably harder.

Franco's decision therefore reduced by one significant country the nations against whom Britain was obliged to fight. Since the United Kingdom's military and naval resources were still scarce, this perhaps enabled British resistance against existing enemies such as Germany and Italy easier to manage. Spanish neutrality, born out of pique towards Hitler, thus proved a boon to Britain's continuing fight.

North Africa: taking the battle to the enemy

When it comes to the battles of 1940–3 in North Africa (also often called the Western Desert), British and Commonwealth writers have written much. American authors have covered it far less, since this is a part of the war as little known in the USA, as Midway and Leyte Gulf are in Europe.

Churchill wanted not only to take the fight to the Axis but also to defend the vital trade links to India (through the Suez Canal) and the all-important oil of the Middle East.

Some background is needed. All of North Africa was ruled by European powers, mostly by France (and the Vichy regime in particular), with Libya an Italian colony and Egypt technically independent, but in practice ruled by Britain. The British also ruled Palestine (now Israel) directly and Jordan and Iraq indirectly. Syria and Lebanon were under Vichy rule until Commonwealth troops seized them at the same time as suppressing a pro-Axis coup in Iraq in 1941. Finally Ethiopia, since its conquest in 1935–36, was also an Italian possession.

Mussolini wanted to expand his empire, and so he dispatched Marshal Graziani to Egypt in September 1940. This proved unsuccessful and in December 1940, the British, with General Sir Archibald Wavell as commander in chief of the Middle East and General Sir Richard O'Connor in charge of the Western Desert Force, launched *Operation Compass*. This was one of the most dramatic and successful campaigns of the war. Within weeks, the Force had taken 400 miles of territory and captured 130,000 Italians. Then another group under Wavell's authority captured

Ethiopia (and what is now Somalia) and Italian East Africa was no more.

It looked as if the British were on a roll. But then, as Evan Mawdsley so aptly puts it, 'Churchill followed his winter victory in Egypt and Cyrenaica (in Libya) with his worst strategic mistake of the war.' He decided to send his victorious armies out of Libya, where they were winning, to help rescue Greece from German attack.

Mussolini had seized Albania back in April 1939. He was keen to have victories of his own, so to Hitler's fury, on 28 October 1940 Italian troops invaded Greece from Albanian soil. The Germans would have preferred their ally to concentrate on fighting the British. Soon, even the best Italian divisions were stuck in the mountains, and Greek resistance proved highly effective.

Hitler, therefore, decided that he needed to send troops both to North Africa (the Afrika Korps) and also to aid the Italians in the Balkans. Both would take time.

Hitler's Balkan change of plan

And then the situation changed. Germany had already pressured both Bulgaria and Romania into client status (each country being far more frightened of Stalin than of Hitler), and Romania, with the massive oil fields at Ploesti, was of inestimable economic importance to the Third Reich. On 25 March 1941, it looked as if German bullying had prevailed in Yugoslavia as well, with the regent, Prince Paul, signing a pact with Hitler. But then on 27 March, there was an SOE-aided coup in Belgrade, with the Yugoslav army deciding to back the Allies instead.

Hitler was speechless and decided that his already planned *Operation Marita* to conquer the Balkans would now include Yugoslavia as well. Within days, Belgrade was bombed into submission and a German army swept through the country in just under a week.

Greece was next on the list. Britain had already sent RAF fighters to help and there were also troops (including those from New Zealand) in Crete. But now the British government and Wavell decided to dispatch 58,000 further troops from North Africa to Greece.

It was, as writers such as Anthony Beevor and Max Hastings have reminded us, another Dunkirk. Two thousand Commonwealth troops were killed or injured and another fourteen thousand were captured, along with an enormous amount of valuable and irreplaceable military hardware. This occurred just as Rommel was landing in North Africa to help the Italians. Greece had been conquered in only three weeks.

Then in May 1941, Crete was captured by airborne German troops. Allied forces had Ultra (see below) but made such errors that the Wehrmacht were able to conquer the island easily, creating yet another ignominious British-led defeat. This time eighteen thousand Allied troops were rescued but nine thousand were abandoned to the Germans and, as before, much vital equipment was lost.

WHEN ULTRA FAILED TO WORK

It is rightly said of Ultra that it helped to shorten the war, and thereby save countless lives. Ultra was the codename for the British ability to break the top-secret German 'Enigma' military ciphers, based at the top decoding signals intelligence station at Bletchley Park, not far from London. Churchill regarded this source as of the greatest importance. It was so clandestine that the story of how the British broke the German codes did not emerge for decades afterwards. (The USA similarly broke the Japanese diplomatic codes, to equally good effect.)

However, such critical intelligence is only as good as the people who use it, and never has this been shown better than by the fiasco in Crete. The New Zealand commander there, General Sir Bernard Freyberg, held the Victoria Cross and was probably one of the most valiant soldiers to hold that decoration.

But he failed totally to make proper use of all the Ultra material, which came to him with complete accuracy on all German intentions for the invasion of Crete, *Operation Merkur*. He persisted, as Anthony Beevor's definitive accounts show us, in believing that the attack would come from the sea. Troops were thus placed in strength in places where no German troops were coming. Instead, they came by air as paratroopers under the command of General Kurt Student. The airfields were woefully defended, and as a result enough Wehrmacht troops were able to land to gain a foothold from which they were then able to conquer the island.

Ultra's intelligence told Freyberg what he needed to know, but he persisted with his own ideas – to complete disaster. Thankfully, as war progressed the Allies had able commanders who knew how best to use the priceless information and insight into the enemy that Ultra gave them.

And a final codicil on the debacle in Crete: it nearly went wrong for the Germans and probably would have done so if the airfields had been guarded with enough troops. The Wehrmacht lost 1,856 paratroopers on the first day of the invasion, and eventually had some 6,000 casualties altogether. Germany decided never to use airborne troops on that scale again, as they deemed the cost too high. The British took the opposite view – paratrooper attacks work, and so the famous Parachute Regiment was born, to the huge advantage of the Allies, especially from D-Day and beyond, the debacle at Arnhem in 1944 notwithstanding.

The price for Britain came swiftly. By the end of April, so successful had Rommel been that Axis forces had wiped out all of the British general Sir Richard O'Connor's hard-fought victories and the Afrika Korps was on the border of Egypt itself.

Many British officers at the time, notably the director of plans, Sir John Kennedy and an understandably embittered O'Connor, the ground commander, knew that Allied aid to Greece was a catastrophe. Either far more troops should have been sent or none at all. As historians have pointed out, Hitler had superb inland lines of communication, from the Third Reich overland through Yugoslavia to Greece, whereas Britain and its Commonwealth allies had to send everything by ship, not just from North Africa but also from the United Kingdom itself. By mid-1941, it looked as if not only had the Allies lost Greece but that they were about to lose the vital possession of Egypt itself. Seldom in war have fortunes turned so quickly.

Setbacks in Africa

The military campaign to win back lost territory proved futile. British troops had been seriously overstretched in any case by the need to capture Syria from Vichy forces and to suppress the revolt in Iraq. In many ways, it was amazing that Rommel's forces did not sweep into Cairo. Just as regrettably, General O'Connor was captured by the Axis on 2 April 1941 and was not able to escape for two years, thus losing Britain an able commander at a time when those of his skill were rare.

Another senior Allied leader also lost his job, but this time through being sacked by Churchill. Those who criticise the prime minister's wartime record point towards his endless tendency to interfere, but in fairness there was probably not much he could do at this stage. He replaced Wavell (exiling him to India, where the later ended up as viceroy in 1943) and substituted General Sir Claude Auchinleck.

The Auk was made of sterner stuff, but with the considerable lack of resources at his disposal there was very little that he could do to tilt the war in favour of the Allies. Not until substantial supplies came from the USA was any real change possible, and by that time, in 1942, the key city of Tobruk, on the Mediterranean coast of Libya, near the border with Egypt, had fallen to Rommel. Churchill's patience with Auchinleck was exhausted. Realistically, victory in the desert would take a long time and patience was not a virtue that Churchill possessed.

The USA to the rescue: America as the arsenal of democracy

However, according to some criteria Churchill was highly successful. Roosevelt's re-election had greatly strengthened the president's hand in dealing with isolationist opinions at home. In his famous 17 December address to the American people, he likened American aid to the besieged British to a generous man giving his hose to a next-door neighbour whose house was on fire. On 30 December, in one of his 'fireside' chats on radio, he defended the idea of lend-lease. This was the plan by which the USA would lend key strategic military assets to the United Kingdom in return for America gaining British economic assets and bases in or near the USA. He called the USA the 'great arsenal of democracy'. So on 8 March 1941, the Senate passed the Lend-Lease Act. This was in fact a glorious circumnavigation around years of neutrality acts that would have forbidden completely what Congress had now authorised Roosevelt to do.

At the time, Churchill hailed this as one of the least sordid (sic) acts of generosity in history. His detractors have pointed out that it was nothing of the kind, since getting some fairly ancient naval destroyers as part of the deal was not exactly a donation of war-winning assets. And in return for equipment the United States effectively stripped bare British economic assets in the USA, along with the right to take over several Royal Naval bases.

This criticism is rather unfair. Back in 1940, Churchill had promised victory 'whatever the cost' and now payment time had come. Britain was bankrupt and could not possibly have continued alone. The USA was not at this time in the war and Roosevelt knew that there was strong sentiment in his own country to continue to stay neutral. It goes without saying that the Americans would drive a hard bargain. They could not throw their own national interest in the bin. What was truly amazing about lend–lease is that Roosevelt was able to obtain it at all. So in 1942, with the USA in the war, Britain was able to receive exactly the kind of military equipment from its American ally that made a critical difference in Britain's ability to fight the war. This was also vital because it was before the USA had been able to bring its own armies up to proper fighting size.

In August 1941, Churchill went to meet Roosevelt at Placentia Bay, in Canadian waters, where they formulated the Atlantic Charter. The USA was still not able to enter the war, but as Roosevelt put it, America was effectively doing everything short of war to help the British survive. Churchill's genius in realising that the New World would come to the rescue of the Old was being vindicated.

THE ATLANTIC CHARTER

Britain and the USA signed an agreement called The Atlantic Charter on 14 August 1941. Strictly speaking it was never co-signed by Churchill and Roosevelt, but in practice it worked as a basis for the aims and aspirations of the two major English-speaking democracies. And we must remember that the USA was still a neutral country, albeit one that was doing all possible within that constraint to make sure that Britain survived.

The eight key points of the Charter can be summarised as follows:

1   No territorial gains were to be sought by the United States or the United Kingdom.
2   Territorial adjustments must be in accord with the wishes of the peoples concerned.
3   All people had a right to self-determination.
4   Trade barriers were to be lowered.
5   There was to be global economic co-operation and advancement of social welfare.
6   The participants would work for a world free of want and fear.
7   The participants would work for freedom of the seas.
8   There was to be disarmament of aggressor nations, and a post-war common disarmament.

Needless to say, point 3 was deeply controversial, since the United Kingdom ruled over a vast colonial empire, most notably over India, a nation that Roosevelt felt strongly should be given its independence. Britain's imperial possessions were to prove a major bone of contention between Churchill and Roosevelt throughout the war. Point 2 was to be completely disregarded between 1943–5 concerning Poland, as Britain and the USA gave in entirely to Stalin on the issue of the new borders of the future Polish state. (Churchill even agreed to the moving westwards of Poland's frontiers with Russia and thence with Germany.)

Nonetheless, once the USA joined in the war after Pearl Harbor, the Atlantic Charter became the de facto list of war aims of the Allies, referred to as the United Nations, with point 8 being the basis of the then future UN that we all know today.

This was a brave voyage for Churchill as the Battle of the Atlantic, the German U-boat campaign to prevent American supplies from reaching Britain (and the USSR after June 1941), was now being waged with increasing ferocity. Many ships were being sunk, and lives and supplies lost.

WHEN WAS THE BATTLE OF THE ATLANTIC FOUGHT?

There are numerous dates for the Battle of the Atlantic, the story of the dauntless convoys who had to avoid being sunk by German U-boat submarines while shipping vital men and material across the Atlantic from North America to Britain and Russia.

Churchill declared the battle's beginning in May 1941, and he feared that it might be one that Britain could lose. Many date it September 1939 to May 1943, the latter being the month when the tide suddenly turned to the Allied advantage after a period of devastating shipping losses to German attack.

British historian P. M. H. Bell argued that one should either date it September 1939 to May 1945, the period of the whole war with Germany, or to its critical turning point between March to May 1943. The latter was the time when Allies were finally able to gain the upper hand, thanks in particular to some spectacularly successful technological advances that made the convoys much safer than before.

In essence, though the naval/submarine conflict lasted the entire war, with the Germans making a technological breakthrough of their own in 1945, this was too late to help them regain the initiative, but very much in time to help NATO design nuclear submarines when the Cold War began not long thereafter.

The desert war

By the summer of 1941, the struggles that the British and other empire armies in North Africa were facing against Rommel's German–Italian army were in reality a sideshow compared to the existential and infinitely bigger battles being fought between the USSR and the Third Reich.

Chronologically, the two wars (Western Desert and Eastern Front) were being fought in tandem, but it is simpler to consider the latter separately until December 1941, when Hitler failed to capture Moscow and the Japanese attacked the USA in Pearl Harbor. Thereafter, there is a strong North Africa/Eastern Front link, since Germany's failures in the USSR meant that Rommel was not able to get many of the supplies he needed to fight the Allies, whereas the USA was able to equip its British ally on a large scale.

The critical factor is that the United Kingdom (and its Indian, New Zealand and Australian allies) was able to hang on and thus prevent the Suez Canal and the Middle Eastern oil fields from falling into Axis hands. This, and the similar success of the Red Army against an overwhelmingly larger enemy, meant that when the USA entered the conflict in December 1941, it had allies with whom it could join in the defeat of the Axis powers, and Germany in particular.

Britain's economy was in tatters and millions of Soviet citizens lay dead. But when Pearl Harbor changed the war, the Axis, having made considerable gains from April 1940 to December 1941, and looking almost invincible, had failed to win. The United Kingdom and the USSR were seriously battered but undefeated. They had survived against one of the most vicious forces that the world had ever seen. Now once again the Americans were coming, as they had done in 1917, and while eventual victory would take until 1945 to achieve, the balance of the war permanently changed.

4
The Eastern Front 1941–1943

Barbarossa, the Axis invasion of the USSR, and probably the biggest military operation in history, began on 22 June 1941. And we should describe it that way deliberately. Not only were there some 3,100,000 German troops but also some 650,000 soldiers from other Axis countries. These included Italy, Romania, Hungary and Slovakia but also Spain, a nation that was carefully not at war with any of the western Allies but was one that shared the visceral anti-Communism of the Nazis.

What we need to remember about Barbarossa

For a long time, *Barbarossa* was a war that was remembered, but at the same time forgotten in the West. D-Day for British and Americans alike, El Alamein for the UK, Midway for the USA: these are the battles that we remember.

But one statistic tells us all that we need to know: Eighty percent of German casualties were on the Eastern Front, the existential conflict unleashed between the two totalitarian giants, the Third Reich and the USSR; and over 27 million Soviet citizens died between 1941–5.

Eighty-five percent of German soldiers who fought in World War II were engaged on the Eastern Front, the epic struggle between the Wehrmacht and the Red Army.

Writers such as Evan Mawdsley reckon that about 300,000 to 350,000 US and UK soldiers died during the war. In terms of total population killed, this represents a massively smaller percentage than that of the Soviets.

For the USSR, the total combined deaths were 27 million or well over fourteen percent of the overall population of the Soviet Union. That is, therefore, well over sixty times as many Soviet citizens – soldiers and civilians alike – killed in relation to the number of British or American deaths directly attributable to the war. It is possible that as many as ten million Red Army soldiers lost their lives between 1941–5.

And, as Norman Davies and Timothy Snyder point out in their important interpretations of the war in Europe (*Europe at War* and *Bloodlands: Europe Between Hitler and Stalin*), we must never forget that the 27 million Soviet citizens who perished were of various ethnic backgrounds, not all Russian. Many millions of the deaths were indeed ethnic Russians, but as Davies and Snyder have demonstrated so convincingly, by far the biggest proportion were from what are now the two independent countries of Ukraine and Belarus, citizens of the USSR but not ethnically Russian at all. It is also worth saying that many of the casualties were from other Soviet republics, such as present-day Kazakhstan or Stalin's original home state of Georgia, to take but two examples.

The other key statistic to recall, as Michael Burleigh has correctly reminded us, is that 189,000 Red Army troops were shot by their own side in order to prevent cowardice or to punish lack of the necessary aggression against the German invader. These deaths were executed either directly by the NKVD themselves – the predecessor organisation to the post-war KGB – or by the 'punishment battalions' of soldiers sent ahead of the main army in order to draw German fire. No other army in World War II had an equivalent, not even the Germans or Japanese, and certainly not any of the Allied armies.

Why is all this important?

Our perceptions of World War II are totally distorted if we forget that by far the bloodiest parts of it were fought with no British or American troops present: only the US–Japan conflict in the Pacific comes even close to the barbarity and scale of the Eastern Front. Most German troops, especially most Wehrmacht casualties, never saw combat against the western Allies: remember only fifteen percent of Germans fought against western forces, a tiny percentage. The popular western view of British or American victories determining the outcome of the struggle against Nazism is thus highly skewed, very important though such battles were to Britain and the USA.

Michael Burleigh and BBC documentary maker Laurence Rees have shown clearly in print and on television, that the Eastern Front was not a struggle between democracy and tyranny, but a fight to the death between two of the worst dictatorships ever seen in human history. It also resulted in a slaughter on a massive scale unknown in history.

Before we look at the actual battles, we shall consider some of the background, and why our perception of the German-Soviet 'Great Patriotic War' is often so distorted, in a way that warps our full understanding of World War II itself.

Why, when its battles make so much of the rest of the war seem like minor sideshows, have we in the West overlooked *Barbarossa*? Surely the reason is political: from 1949–91 we were in a state of Cold War with the Soviet Union, with the unthinkable threat of nuclear annihilation always hanging over us if cold war ever became hot. The USSR was not an enemy like Nazi Germany, but it was no friend either, and its intense suffering in what they call the Great Patriotic War was something of which we heard little and knew even less. And at the same time, that very loss was used by the Soviets as the excuse to invade and then subjugate the Iron Curtain countries from 1945–89, with a Russian T34 tank proudly displayed in major cities as the justification for decades of what was in effect alien Russian colonial rule.

The Cold War also meant that we could not see any of the Soviet archives, which described the course of the war, and also the many German archives that had been captured in 1944–5 and kept secret in the USSR, inaccessible to western historians.

In the 1980s, Mikhail Gorbachev began to allow Soviet archives to be seen, and we could begin to piece together the true horrors of the Eastern Front, with even more records becoming open after the end of Communism in 1991.

As often happens, academics were the first to start looking at the archives, followed by enterprising documentary makers, before the results of the new research entered popular consciousness. Television series like *War of the Century* by Laurence Rees showed millions of viewers in the West for the first time the sheer scale and depth of the carnage of 1941–5, the unimaginable atrocities committed mainly by the Germans but also by the Soviets, and the fact that from 1939–41 the Third Reich and USSR were de facto allies, at the cost of the murder of tens of thousands of innocent Poles and other subjugated peoples.

Something like twenty-five percent of the entire population of Belarus died in the war, and about five to six million Ukrainian

THE HUNGER PLAN

We all know of the Holocaust, the Nazi plan to kill all of Europe's Jews but their Hunger Plan is less familiar, even though it was discovered by the Allies in 1945.

The German leadership realised that sending over three million troops into the USSR for *Barbarossa* needed far more food than the Third Reich itself could ever hope to supply. So their solution, historians Lizzie Collingham and Alex Kay have discovered, was to starve thirty million people to death in the conquered territories, with the entire Wehrmacht thereby being able to be fed by Ukrainian grain by 1944. Such was the Hunger Plan drawn up before *Barbarossa* by Herbert Backe, a state secretary responsible to Hermann Göring for the Four Year Plan.

As one of the memoranda put it, if the Wehrmacht was to eat properly, as 'a result, what is necessary for us is extracted from the land, tens of millions will doubtlessly starve to death'. In the conquered region planned for German settlement, most of the Slavic inhabitants 'will have to face the most terrible famine... Many tens of millions of people in this territory will become superfluous and will have to die...'

To SS leader Erich von dem Bach-Zelewski, the number needed to starve was more precise: the aim should be the 'decimation of the Slavic population by thirty million'. This was confirmed by one of the SS commanders attempting to capture Moscow later in 1941, Professor Franz Six: in the territories to be conquered, 'a "blazing strip" will emerge in which all life is to be erased. It is intended to decimate the around thirty million Russians living in this strip through starvation, by removing all foodstuffs from this enormous territory'.

Thankfully, not all the Wehrmacht were barbaric enough to want to implement this policy. But it was carried out thoroughly with most of the Red Army prisoners of war: 3.3 million prisoners (of the 5.7 million captured) were starved to death during 1941–45. Around one million inhabitants of Leningrad starved to death during the siege of that city, and maybe as many as 4.2 million Soviet civilians died of German-created hunger during the war.

civilians died, which is as large a number as the Jews from not just Ukraine who died in the Holocaust.

Since Stalin's pre-war ideological campaigns in that region had already murdered 3.3 million Ukrainians, starved to death in the Great Hunger of the 1930s, that means that what is now Ukraine lost up to ten million people butchered by Stalin and then Hitler, a death toll quite beyond the imagination and effectively within the space of just over a single decade.

The invasion begins

On 22 June 1941 at 4.15 a.m. Moscow time, the greatest war in history began with a massive German bombardment. Three German army groups, north, centre and south, began the invasion of the USSR, known as *Operation Barbarossa*. Three entire Soviet field armies were wiped out within days – General Pavlov was made a scapegoat and shot, but in reality, with Stalin having been in denial until the last minute about the invasion, there was nothing that any Red Army commander could have done to prevent the onslaught that was now taking place. For a brief while, it looked as if Stalin was having some kind of nervous breakdown, since he retreated to his dacha and had to be coaxed back into taking charge.

Did *Marita* delay *Barbarossa*?

One of the greatest myths of World War II is that the need to invade and punish Yugoslavia in April 1941 crucially delayed *Barbarossa*. That delay, it used to be argued, made the crucial difference between the Wehrmacht's success and failure by postponing the attack until the Germans were unable to get far enough to capture Moscow in December 1941.

Significantly, this was a myth propagated both by Hitler, in his rants to his followers as the war ended, and by Churchill in his own war memoirs. In both cases, their arguments were excuses: Hitler's for the failure to conquer Russia and Churchill's for sending troops to Greece so disastrously, and thereby throwing away victory in North Africa in 1941.

However, the tendency is now to say that in fact *Operation Marita*, the German Balkan campaign, made no difference at all to *Barbarossa*. Delays were going to happen anyway, almost all logistical, such as the need for enough transport. It would, therefore,

have been June regardless of the need to secure the Balkans. And
many British soldiers, such as the War Office's director of military
operations, General Sir John Kennedy, felt the same – and he had
served with British troops fighting alongside the anti-Bolshevik
Whites in Russia in 1919–20.

Many argue now that *Barbarossa* was doomed from the start,
and it was never going to succeed; therefore, the exact starting
date does not make much difference. Part of this new view is that
Russian resistance and the sheer enormity of the USSR is what
made German defeat inevitable. It is unfair on the Red Army to
say that it was winter slush that stood between German victory
and defeat.

Nevertheless, Anthony Beevor has a point: seeing Hitler go
south to attack the Balkans persuaded Stalin that a German invasion of the USSR was not going to take place in 1941. This helps
to explain the mystery of why Stalin was so dogged in refusing to
believe all intelligence reports that truthfully told of an imminent
Axis attack – he simply did not believe that that was what Hitler
was going to do. One can say that the real effect of *Marita* was to
lull the Soviet dictator into a false sense of security, with devastating results for his country when *Barbarossa* finally began.

The bulk of the existing Red Air Force was destroyed on the
ground. The Soviets had put their armed services very far forward,
following their invasion of Poland in 1939 – they weren't able to
hold fortified positions against a German attack that Stalin was
certain would never happen. Eighteen hundred Soviet aircraft
were destroyed, and only 330 of the Luftwaffe.

Only in the south was there any real Soviet resistance, and
even there the defending armies were forced back into ignominious retreat. The Red Army was able to make a brief stand around
Smolensk, a town on the Dnieper river, but this too failed. Three
quarters of a million Soviet prisoners of war were taken defending the city in mid-August in what the Germans called a 'Kesselschlacht', or 'cauldron battle'. But 100,000 Red Army troops
escaped the encirclement, and were able to fight another day.

The onslaught, and devastation of the Soviet countryside, seemed to be heading in an inevitable direction. Indeed, by the end of September the Wehrmacht had managed to charge through 440 miles of Soviet territory within just six weeks. It was not surprising that many in Germany thought that the war would soon be over.

This seems to have been a prognosis held in Britain as well, with few generals giving the Soviets a chance of survival. Churchill did his best, sending precious supplies to the USSR. He did so despite decades of anti-Communism going back to his passionate denunciations of the Bolshevik Revolution in 1917 and active advocacy of Western intervention on the side of the Whites against the Reds in the civil war that followed in the early 1920s. But now Stalin's USSR was the enemy of Britain's enemy, and old ideological rancour was put aside in the cause of anti-Nazi solidarity. Eventually, Roosevelt extended lend-lease to the Soviets as well, with many of these supplies going through Siberia unhindered by the Japanese, to Hitler's fury.

But if people in the West thought that the Soviets had no chance of survival, they were wrong.

The Soviets fight back

Let us look at two quotations, both from German commander General Franz Halder, which show why *Barbarossa* failed, and why the new generation of historians such as David Stahel, may well be right to say that the invasion was doomed from the very beginning, let alone being defeated by the winter weather in 1941.

On 3 July 1941, Halder wrote in his diary:

On the whole one can already now say that the objective to destroy the mass of the Russian army in front of the Dvina and Dnieper has been accomplished. I do not doubt... that eastward [of those rivers] we would only have to contend with partial enemy forces, not strong enough to hinder the realisation of the German operational plan. Thus is it probably not an exaggeration when I claim that the campaign against Russia was won within fourteen days.

But then look what he writes in his diary just a few weeks later, on 11 August:

Regarding the general situation, it stands out more and more clearly that we underestimated the Russian colossus... This statement refers just as much to organisational as to economic strengths, to traffic management, above all to pure military potential. At the start of the war we reckoned with 200 enemy divisions. Now we already count 360.

Indeed, he was more correct than we knew. When the invasion began, the USSR had reserves of fourteen million men who could be asked to fight. When *Barbarossa* began on 22 June, Red Army strength stood at 5,373,000. By the end of August, there were 6,889,000 soldiers, despite gigantic losses at the outset of the war to the invaders. By the end of the year, best reckonings put the total Red Army strength at eight million. This is despite the fact that in June to September alone the Red Army had lost over two million men (most of whom became prisoners of war, only to be deliberately malnourished and starved to death by their German captors), with 665,000 such losses at the Battle of Kiev alone.

As Anthony Beevor writes, the 'Kiev *Kesselschlacht* was the largest in military history. German morale soared again.' The situation for the Soviets looked hopeless as mid-September saw the invaders looking and feeling invincible.

But this would be highly misleading. For whenever Soviet troops were wiped out or captured, more came to replace them.

This means that a loss of two million was counterbalanced by a net increase of over two and a half million new Red Army soldiers in the early months of the war. July 1941 saw no fewer than thirteen new Soviet field armies being created, and a further fourteen entire armies in August.

Why the Germans were already losing

Meanwhile, in June to September, the Wehrmacht lost 185,000 soldiers, which was more than the 102,000 they had lost in the entire war before *Barbarossa* began. And while the Luftwaffe lost 1,290 planes during the Battle of Britain, it lost 2,180 in 1941 over the USSR. And remember, the Luftwaffe had wiped out most of the existing Red Air Force planes on the ground within days of the invasion being launched.

The rest of Halder's diary for 11 August, written before the Wehrmacht capture of Kiev a month later, is equally revealing:

> These [360 Red Army] Divisions are not armed and equipped in our sense and tactically they are inadequately led in many ways. But they are there and when we destroy a dozen of them, then the Russians put another dozen in their place. The time factor favours them, as they are near to their own centres of power, while we are always moving further away from ours.

This is the same point that Paul Kennedy and others have made in talking both about the Nazi invasion of the Soviet Union and the Japanese attack against the Americans in the Pacific: distance is all important in war.

As Evan Mawdsley has pointed out, 'the destruction of the Soviet Western Army Group [in June to July 1941] was operationally as devastating as the entrapment of the French and British armies north of the Somme in 1940'. But whereas, one could add, that led to the subsequent collapse of France within weeks, and German victory, in the USSR the war went on… and on… and on….

For as historians remind us, the breadth of the Anglo-French-German front in 1940 was 150 miles, but in *Barbarossa* it was 750 miles, five times greater. The Germans only had to go 75 miles to Paris in 1940, but from the Dvina–Dnieper rivers to Moscow was 350 miles.

This was Halder's epiphany moment. As he concluded, even in August, with the Wehrmacht feeling invincible:

> And so our troops, spread over an immense front line, without any depth, are subject to the incessant attacks of the enemy. They are sometimes successful, because in these enormous spaces far too many gaps must be left open.

The bottom line is that while the Russians had an endless supply of replacement troops, the Wehrmacht had virtually none, first because there were simply not enough German males to replace those lost by attrition. Additionally, the Third Reich was seriously overstretched, having to guard a vast empire from Norway in northwest Europe to Greece in the southeast. For the Soviets, however, fighting a one-front war, and with an exponentially bigger population base, that simply was not a problem.

While even the new wave of historians on the Eastern Front do not mention it, we have already seen in Khalkhin Gol in 1939 and will see when we look at Japan's entry into the war in December 1941 the crucial fact of the war: Stalin was of course able to send troops from Siberia, away from the border with Japan and to do this because of the neutrality agreement that he had signed in April 1941 with the Japanese. Trusting the Japanese to keep their side of the bargain, the Soviets could, as we saw, put the whole bulk of their armed forces into the conflict against Germany. So once again, the Soviet–Japanese relationship played a major part in the outcome of World War II.

This is why the new wave of historians argue that *Barbarossa* was logistically doomed from the beginning – the Germans simply did not have the ability to conquer over such vast and impenetrable distances.

HORSES AND EXHAUSTED INVADERS

Much has been written about frostbitten German troops freezing in inadequate uniforms as they retreated from the Moscow Front in late 1941.

But in fact large numbers of them were already exhausted in the summer, when things were supposed to be going well for them.

As one German commander wrote as early as July, 'Yesterday our regiment marched 54, [today] another 47km. To do that once is possible. To do that having already had numerous marches of 30-40 km with more to come, that is something else...' And as a wretched infantry soldier put it after such strain:

> We're wet through all over, sweat is running down our faces in wide streams – not just sweat, but sometimes tears too, tears of helpless rage, desperation, and pain, squeezed out of us by this inhuman effort.

And a key statistic: the Germans had 750,000 transport horses as part of their invasion force, not the technology of the mid-twentieth century but that of ages past. Despite their supposed speed of attack, one historian has worked out that it took Napoleon less time to reach the key city of Smolensk in 1812 than it did the Wehrmacht in 1941.

Barbarossa may have been many things, but blitzkrieg it was not.

Hitler divides his forces – but maybe the war is already lost?

Whether or not it was right to go for Moscow, as many of Hitler's commanders would have done, or south to Ukraine and the rich agricultural areas of the USSR, is a moot point. For some generals it was either Moscow or Ukraine, and for others both the capital and the grainfields. In the end, the Wehrmacht got the worst of both worlds, with an initial diversion of Army Group South to Ukraine, and then a decision to go for Moscow after all. Hitler had economic motives for going south, with both grain and oil being vital to the German war effort. While this made no strategic sense to his generals it does make sense if one realises that Germany's supplies were so limited that new sources were always necessary if the war was to continue.

As we saw, the move south was a success, with German soldiers reaching as far as the river Don, and most of Ukraine captured. However, the invaders did not manage to get down as far as the Caucasus and to the rich oil wells there. And the racist policy of the Nazis made a vast difference, to the frustration of many of the Wehrmacht leadership.

With three million Ukrainians starved to death, many in that region welcomed the Germans as liberators. But while many of them went on to join some form of the SS (many of the concentration camp guards were Ukrainians), Hitler's racial policy, and his determination to regard all Slavs as lesser human beings, remained non-negotiable and absolute, to the great cost of the invaders.

In retrospect, this seems a crazy decision – until one remembers that the doctrine of Aryan superiority, and the need to have areas such as Ukraine as resettlement regions for racially pure Germans, was the very essence of Nazi ideology. The Germans had been pro-Ukrainian in 1918 and had done everything possible to foster an independence movement during World War I. But in 1941, it was Nazis invading the Soviet Union, and a policy of supporting Ukrainian anti-Russian nationalism was against all that Nazism stood for and propagated. Once again, Nazi beliefs and the way in which they had, by 1941, permeated even the Wehrmacht, showed that Germany had shot itself in the foot even before *Barbarossa* had begun.

The fight for Moscow

With much of Ukraine conquered and Kiev fallen, Hitler now allowed his soldiers their prime aim – the capture of Moscow. This battle was launched in September 1941 as *Operation Typhoon*. It began well for the Germans, since they came up against inexperienced Red Army troops. Often forgotten is a great Wehrmacht victory, the Battle of Viaz'ma–Briansk, in which 760,000 Soviet troops were captured, or seventy entire Red Army divisions.

But now a crucial difference between Hitler and Stalin emerged. Both men were vile dictators, happy to shed the blood of millions (and up to 1941, Stalin's death count had been much larger). However, while Hitler insisted on having his own way with his military subordinates, Stalin now understood that he needed urgently to listen to his generals – although his overall authority remained undiminished. Zhukov, whom many now reckon was the greatest commander of World War II, was put in charge of the Western Army Group.

The Soviet capital could have been transferred to Kuibyshev (now Samara), a town on the Volga river some 539 miles from Moscow. A train was prepared to take Stalin and a bunker built ready for his use. But Stalin took the key decision to stay in Moscow for morale, and the entire population was mobilised to defend it against what was expected to be an imminent attack. NKVD troops were employed to shoot deserters or shirkers and

375,000 ethnic Germans – the first of a series of vast deporta-
tions – were sent east.

The cult of Stalin now began in even more earnest than
before the war. This was now the great patriotic war, with all
Soviet citizens enlisted in the struggle – and as Stalin realised, a
battle for survival, for as he broadcast to his fellow Muscovites in
celebration of the Bolshevik Revolution, the 'German invaders
want a war of extermination. Very well then, they shall have one!'

By 30 November, the advance guard of Army Group Centre,
the Third Panzer Army, was a mere forty kilometres from
Moscow itself, and the Fourth Panzer just sixteen away. But the
temperature was now nearly -20C, and the German armies were
nowhere near prepared enough for that level of cold.

Then on 6 December 1941, the Red Army counteroffensive,
under Zhukov's command, began. Four new armies launched the
attack, all of course fully prepared to fight in winter and with
tanks and weaponry built to withstand the icy weather conditions. By contrast, German soldiers who fell asleep on sentry duty
often froze to death. Moscow was safe with the Germans pushed
back well over fifty miles.

Evan Mawdsley has suggested that the 'Battle of Moscow,
more than the Battle of Stalingrad, marked the turning point
of the war. On 8 December, Hitler secretly admitted that the
offensive was – for the moment – over.' All three Army Group
commanders were sacked.

But Mawdsley makes an even more important point:

> It was not that the Germans failed to get to Moscow
> before the weather broke; rather they were caught by
> the freeze because they had failed to reach Moscow. Also,
> it was not that they lost the Battle of Moscow because
> they had a chaotic command structure; rather, they had a
> chaotic command structure because they lost the Battle
> of Moscow.

HOW THE GERMANS COULD HAVE CONQUERED THE USSR

Much has been written about the most successful Soviet comm-ander 'General Winter' and how the arctic conditions by the end of 1941 changed the outcome of the invasion. The failure of the Germans to capture Moscow by the beginning of December, and their subsequent need to retreat up to 150 miles and more was certainly very influential. Others have referred to the snow and slush – the 'rasputitsa' – which made fighting terrible not just in the winter but also in the spring, with all the melting ice making transport and logistics almost impossible. Well known too is the fact that most German soldiers in the winter of 1941–42 had no cold-weather clothes, and so many froze to death, a product of Hitler's arrogance in thinking that the war would have already been won and over.

All this is true and vital, but perhaps it is not quite that simple. The Germans were hindered by their racial ideology that condemned all Slavs as lesser human beings. It never occurred to them that the Red Army could produce troops as effective as the Wehrmacht, capable both of resisting the invasion and of fighting back. In 1918, when German troops had previously occupied this region, they sought local collaborators. This time they treated everyone as an enemy, with devastating results.

The fact that Stalin could send fresh troops from the Far East to fight the invaders was something the Germans never properly fathomed. This, coupled with the considerable German intelligence blunders that led them vastly to underestimate the Red Army, made the Germans even more vulnerable.

The sheer size of the USSR – surely the most important factor of all – meant that the kind of successful blitzkrieg the Germans employed against comparatively smaller countries such as France was simply impossible logistically in a country massively larger such as the Soviet Union.

All these four factors must be added in to the normal reasons why the Germans were not successful. The USSR was no Low Coun-tries or France, and what is perhaps amazing is not that the Germans almost got as far as Moscow but that they were able against all the odds to reach as far into Russia at all.

(See also the Box on Horses and exhausted invaders.)

Was the invasion now doomed?

The internal chaos of the German command system therefore meant that the invasion was destined not to succeed in the long term. But if the new thesis of David Stahel and others is true, the war had already been lost by August, long before the ice and rasputitsa slush, since the dusty roads in the summer had already had a devastating effect on the panzers, rendering many of them useless without a shot being fired. If that is the case, then *Barbarossa* was doomed from the beginning.

And as we shall see, December 1941 was the turning point for another reason: the USA had entered the war. Germany did not begin to have the resources to fight both the USA and the USSR at the same time, so the German failure outside Moscow was now to prove fatal for the Third Reich.

Hitler had failed in 1940 to conquer Britain. In 1941, he failed again with the USSR, even though he took millions of Soviet lives in the attempt. Now the world's greatest power was against him. The war would have another four terrible years to run, including the deaths of further millions of innocent civilians in the process.

Fell Blau – Hitler's next attempt at conquest

Operation Blue (Fell Blau) was the first time that Hitler's decision to override his military commanders led to catastrophic defeat. Part of the Hitler myth among his people and even his military commanders was that he was a genius whose gambler's instincts led him to resounding victories when his more cautious generals had failed. One could argue that his prevarication in 1941 – Moscow or Ukraine or both simultaneously – had been a critical mistake. But in 1942, his luck had in a sense returned, and the Wehrmacht, while no longer after Moscow, was able to penetrate far further into Soviet territory than ever before.

The scale of the Eastern Front, from the Arctic Circle in the north to the Caucasus mountains in the south, was hundreds of miles long. This in itself did not bode well for Germany. Yet *Operation Blue* started very well indeed for the Wehrmacht.

The attacks began on 28 June, on a front no less than 350 miles wide. As Evan Mawdsley rightly points out, the Battle of the Don [river] Bend is a 'major forgotten event of World War II… [The Red Army] lost 2500 tanks and 370,000 men.' On 14 July, the vital town of Rostov-on-Don was captured and the way to the Caucasus was opened. However, not all was going entirely to the original German plan. Stalin, having now realised that Moscow was not going to be attacked after all, understood that he needed to enable his commanders to escape encirclement by the Germans.

On 23 July, Hitler decided to divide his force into two – Army Group A would go for the Caucasus and the vitally needed oil wells, and Army Group B, under General Paulus, would attack along the Volga, with the capture of Stalingrad among its key aims.

Army Group A was soon achieving astonishing things. There was even fear again, as in December 1941, that the USSR would be finished, since the disaster in the Crimea also bode badly for Soviet survival. Hitler proceeded to take command of the group himself, and victory seemed assured. Specialist German troops even took control of Mount Elbrus, the highest peak in the Caucasus and waved the Third Reich battle flag.

German troops from Army Group A did manage to penetrate as far as the key oil town of Maikop, much of which had been destroyed. But this was all hubris, since on 31 August, Field Marshal List told Hitler that the troops could go no further. They had been completely overstretched.

As Anthony Beevor correctly says:

A grossly over-extended Wehrmacht, relying excessively on weak allies, was now doomed to lose its great advantage of *Bewegungskrieg* – a war of movement. That era was finished, because the Germans had finally lost their initiative…. Hitler had begun to suspect that the high water mark of the Third Reich's expansion had been reached.

Indeed it had – with 'exhausted troops and unsustainable supply lines'. And now, with Army Group B at Stalingrad, the Germans would discover how shatteringly true that had become.

Stalingrad: an iconic battle now rages

Stalingrad is one of the iconic battles of World War II. Historians have argued since that some battles were in fact more important – such as that of Kursk fought in 1943 – but it is unquestionably Stalingrad that has entered the popular imagination and with excellent reason. While the 2001 film *Enemy At The Gates* has been criticised for lack of historical accuracy, it does give an excellent picture of the sheer horror and the scale of carnage that characterised the conflict, between August 1942 and the formal German surrender on 30 January 1943 (with some soldiers fighting on until February).

Stalingrad was once Tsaritsyn, and its change of name made it into a special place for the Soviet dictator, and thus an equally symbolic city for the Germans to capture. In one sense, this was a major problem because most military analysts now consider that Army Group B under Paulus would have been far better employed passing it by and continuing further to take more easily conquerable land beyond the city. But Hitler decreed otherwise and from then on the doom of hundreds of thousands of German troops was sealed.

Nearly two million Soviet soldiers alone were engaged on the various fronts. According to whose statistics one believes, some 1,150,000 of them were killed or wounded, along with at least 40,000 civilians who died during the siege. At least 850,000 Germans were wounded or killed, and of those thousands taken prisoner, very few survived the terror of Soviet prison camps to return home in 1955.

Much of the fighting in Stalingrad was street-by-street, and often hand-to-hand. The sheer level of winter cold did not help the German invaders, many of whom froze or starved. Hitler forbade the Sixth Army to retreat and Stalin similarly forbade the Red Army to move.

However, what really made the difference was the realisation of Zhukov and the Red Army that the Germans fighting in Stalingrad could be completely surrounded, cut off and vanquished. What turned the tide therefore was not so much the fighting within the city itself – the main aim of which was to keep the Germans in place – but many miles away, in the Red Army's great offensive, *Operation Uranus*.

It was that brilliant move against the Axis forces, many of whom were ill-trained and ineffective Romanians and Italians that won the conflict for the USSR. Well over a million Soviet troops were able to surround and entrap the German army completely in Stalingrad. Other German units, such as those under the command of General Hoth, were entirely unable to break through to the beleaguered Sixth Army, who now found themselves at least seventy-five miles away from friendly Wehrmacht forces.

This also meant that the Luftwaffe proved utterly unable to supply the Germans in Stalingrad. The latter fought heroically on but in increasingly hopeless circumstances, forbidden to retreat by Hitler's orders.

At Leningrad also, the other renowned battle, the German siege, while not fully over, suffered a major blow. Two Soviet armies ended the encirclement of the city and on 18 January Zhukov, the Russian commander on temporary assignment to help alleviate the siege there, became a Marshal of the Soviet Union.

On 30 January 1943, Hitler promoted Paulus to the similar rank of Field Marshal. No one holding this rank had ever surrendered, and Hitler hoped, in barbaric fashion, that Paulus would either fight to the bitter end or commit suicide. But Paulus did neither. He recognised the inevitable at Stalingrad and surrendered the next day, 31 January, with ignominy. Those German soldiers who had survived winter and slaughter were now carted off to an uncertain fate as prisoners of war.

Stalin had won his iconic victory. Stalingrad, the city named after him, was saved. While the Red Army would soon go on to win even greater battles, the psychological advantage had now shifted on the Eastern Front to them and away from the now clearly beatable Germans. And the situation at Leningrad had improved too.

The aftermath of the German Stalingrad defeat

Stalingrad was the worst German defeat so far in the war. While the Wehrmacht had been obliged to retreat considerably elsewhere from its peak 1942 positions in the USSR, this was the first time that a whole German army had been forced to surrender. The Japanese, looking at Russian film of the event, suddenly began to wonder if their supposedly invincible Nazi allies really were the all-conquering master race after all. But the key thing, as Evan Mawdsley has rightly observed, was that in the 'last analysis…. Hitler did not lose the Battle of Stalingrad; the Red Army won it'.

The British were so impressed by the Soviet success that King George VI, via Churchill, was to give Stalin a special Stalingrad sword. While winning battles in North Africa against the Germans was good news for Churchill, it was nothing compared to the heroic status that Stalingrad conferred on Stalin himself, who was soon able to award himself the post of Marshal of the Soviet Union. From now on, Hitler had no lasting victories on the Eastern Front, and while millions more Red Army troops and Soviet civilians would die before the fall of Berlin in May 1945, one could say that the die was cast. *Operation Uranus* and the linked *Operation Little Saturn* cost vast numbers of Soviet lives, but Zhukov and his fellow Red Army commanders were on the road to eventual victory, and in their case, it was victory whatever the cost, at a price so high that we can scarcely take it in.

The Russians were now able to launch a counteroffensive, one that would soon put them in a dangerously overextended position. In the south, *Operation Little Saturn* enabled them to advance so fast – the Red Army captured Kharkov for example – that they made the same mistake as the Germans had in 1941 and pushed themselves too far forward.

General Manstein, the great veteran of the conquest of France, was now in command in this region of Wehrmacht forces, and in March 1943 he launched a very successful counter-attack response to the Red Army counteroffensive. Kharkov was retaken. The Germans realised that they could perhaps now regain huge amounts of lost territory and stop the overextended Russians in their tracks. The battle lines for the struggle of the Kursk Salient had now begun to be drawn.

Kursk: a titanic battle between tanks and planes

The battle of Kursk has been called the greatest ever tank battle in history. Because historians love to counter exaggerated claims this description has been called into question. But surely Anthony Beevor (whose account of the various military engagements that took place from July to August 1943 should be read by all those interested in detailed descriptions) is right to say that this was the biggest tank and air battle in history, since the vicious aerial combat between the Soviet and German air forces was also pivotal in deciding who finally won.

The sheer scale of the operations that took place from July to August 1943 in this part of the USSR is overwhelming. For not only was there the Battle of Kursk itself, but the Soviet counteroffensive *Operation Kutuzov* and then the massive battles for the recapture of Orel and Kharkov as well. In just the German offensive at Kursk (*Operation Citadel* or *Zitadelle*) there were over 1,900,000 Red Army forces facing nearly 780,000 German troops. As with so many of the battles of the Eastern Front, parallel events elsewhere (such as the Allied invasion of Sicily at the same time) are dwarfed by comparison.

While people outside the USSR think of Kursk in isolation, as a battle on its own, it was in fact, from the Soviet viewpoint, merely part one of the proceedings. Significantly, they had two sources of sigint (signals intelligence) information on German intentions – those supplied officially by the Allies and those given unofficially by one of their key spies in Britain, the traitor John Cairncross, who was working both for British intelligence and for the NKVD at the same time. (He was later to use the material he gave to the Soviets as justification for his years of treachery.)

For Hitler, the attack on the Soviet bulge, or salient, around Kursk was a gambler's last desperate attempt at a successful throw. Most sensible Germans now understood that an actual conquest of the USSR was impossible. But a counter-thrust that regained the initiative lost at Stalingrad, and that one final attempt to get down to the oil fields in the Caucasus was, he and his generals felt, worth a try. Since the Red Army's forward position could be surrounded and cut off at Kursk, it was decided to try this. But Hitler proved, as ever, his own worst enemy. Planning began in March 1943, but while a major offensive could have been launched as early as May, because Hitler wanted the new Panther tank in operation, he postponed the actual assault until July.

This proved ideal for the Red Army, and for Zhukov and the other senior Soviet marshals and generals involved in planning the Soviet reaction. Since they had accurate intelligence on what the Germans were doing, they were able to build a massive defensive front, with ditches, some 6,000 miles of tunnels, traps and with plenty of hidden units ready to counter-attack when necessary. And this time Stalin agreed with his commanders that the Germans should be deceived into thinking that they had the initiative.

Well over 6,000 tanks took part when the Kursk operations finally began on 5 July 1943. At some stages during the fighting, it was literally tank-to-tank and even man-to-man. As Anthony Beevor brilliantly brings out, the sheer noise and scale of the carnage was such that no one had seen its like before, with the din of tank combat, rocket attacks and the aerial war driving soldiers actually insane on the battlefield (one poor German soldier started to dance the can-can from mental collapse until rescued by comrades). The key thing, too, is that it was as much a battle between fighter pilots as between tanks, and as it took some days for the Soviets to gain air superiority, the carnage from air attacks on ground troops was colossal.

The first battle – for control of the Kursk bulge or salient – came finally to a halt as it became apparent that the Germans had failed to break through, despite their tanks and the fact that many of their divisions were elite SS panzer units notorious for their fanaticism.

The difference that Kursk made

Here in Kursk the war elsewhere did make a difference. Hitler had wanted Kursk to show what his forces could still accomplish

– that they should be 'a beacon seen around the world'. Their failure proved otherwise. But not only that, the Allied landings in Sicily, although a sideshow in comparison, worried him considerably. Fearful that he might lose Italy, he took the fateful decision (between 13 and 17 July) to withdraw key divisions from the Eastern Front to the Mediterranean. Just as his troops in the USSR needed all that they could get, he deprived them of a key SS panzer division and more besides.

This was important because on 12 July the Soviet counter-offensive, *Operation Kutuzov,* had begun. Like the great Russian commander in the war against Napoleon for whom it was named, it was equally successful at repelling the invaders. Then on 3 August, *Operation Rumyanstsev* was unleashed, with just under one million Soviet troops and almost 2,500 tanks. By 5 August, Orel had been recaptured, and on 28 August, even Kharkov fell back into Soviet hands. The Germans had been comprehensively defeated.

However, the German losses had been fewer than that of the Red Army. If one adds up the losses in all three phases of the conflict (Kursk and the two Soviet offensives) they are catastrophic. Overall, Soviet casualties were around 863,000 and the Germans' 203,000 with the Red Army losing five to six times as many tanks as the Wehrmacht and SS.

The difference was that, whereas such inconceivable losses could not be made up or replaced by the Germans, this was far from the case with the USSR. As with the early days of *Barbarossa,* German panzer commanders in 1943 would write home that they would destroy an entire Soviet division only to see another one come up to replace them and launch an attack.

But as Evan Mawdsley correctly concludes, the 'battle was, however, a German defeat… at best a greater German success at Kursk would simply have delayed the Soviet offensive. The Battles of Moscow and Stalingrad were much more significant turning points.' Which battle serves as the turning point is much debated. But whichever engagement one chooses it is clear that by now there was no way back for Germany.

From now on, the Red Army juggernaut would prove all-powerful. Victory for Stalin was a matter of time, and the fact that it still took nearly two more years, until May 1945, to achieve, with millions more slaughtered, is proof of how truly terrible the war had become.

KEY MOMENTS, OR BATTLES ALONG THE WAY

Most of us were brought up to regard certain events as key battles of World War II, their names depending often upon in which country we were born. British people tend to look nostalgically at victories against German troops that took place before the USA became a major player in the war. Americans often look to battles in the Pacific, with the USA fighting the Japanese, and in which no other nations took part. This is quite natural but it is also misleading.

Now our broader understanding of history has shifted as people have realised that the epic struggles of the war in fact took place elsewhere. Moscow in 1941, Stalingrad, the Battle of Kursk – all of these Eastern Front clashes involved far more men than most of the battles fought by the Western Allies and can therefore claim to be much more important than even D-Day, the nearest that Western forces came to the gigantic scale of the Soviet–German conflagrations in which millions of troops took part.

But more radical questions are now being asked. Were any of these titanic battles turning points in the war? Or did the Allies win incrementally, through small but deeply significant victories, many of them technological in nature, none of which were individually important but which cumulatively ensured the defeat of the Axis?

We will look later at many of these achievements, such as the transformative fighter plane, the P-51 Mustang, elsewhere. And there is no question that they made a major difference to winning the war.

But while the idea that boffins and engineers won the war is persuasive, surely some of the traditional view, that key battles really did count, still holds? If the United Kingdom had lost the Battle of Britain, the UK would have fallen to Hitler and the war would have been drastically different. An American loss at Midway or the capture of Moscow by the Wehrmacht might not have altered the eventual outcome of the war, but its course would have been far longer and considerably bloodier.

And perhaps both sides of the argument are right? The P-51 and the Seabees (or CBs, the US Navy Construction Battalions) helped massively to shorten the war by giving the Allies the key technical edge over their enemies. German failure to seize Moscow and Japanese defeat at Midway halted the Axis expansion in its tracks. Technology and individual battles proved pivotal and showed that however powerful Germany and Japan might have seemed in the early part of the war, Allied victory was bound to happen sooner or later. Thanks to unsung engineers, brilliant Soviet commanders and American admirals, this victory was achieved in much less time than would have been the case otherwise.

5

The Asian and Pacific War 1941–1943

The Soviet–Japanese non-aggression pact and its consequences

When historians think of April 1941, it is usually in the context of German armies pouring through and dismembering Yugoslavia, on the way to conquering Greece. As we noted earlier, 13 April 1941 is one of the most important dates in the war, but for a quite different reason. On that day, the Japanese-Soviet Non-Aggression Pact was signed, a five-year treaty in which both Japan and the USSR promised not to invade one another and to remain neutral in each other's wars.

Until the Soviet Union attacked the Japanese Kwantung Army in Manchuria on 9 August 1945 (a day better known for the second atomic bomb dropped on Nagasaki), both countries stuck firmly to the last letter of their agreement. Stalin refused to help the Allies against Japan, and the Japanese, to German fury, allowed American lend-lease supplies to come unhindered and in vast quantities to aid the USSR's struggle against the Third Reich.

This treaty, the natural conclusion to the Japanese mauling by Soviet troops at Khalkhin Gol (or Nomonhan) in 1939, changed the entire course of the war.

This made the critical difference between defeat and victory for the USSR, because if the Japanese had taken the northern option and invaded Siberia in June 1941 in conjunction with Hitler's invasion of the Soviet west, the USSR's very survival could have been in doubt. Invasions of Russia from Europe have always failed, but the Mongol attack from the east succeeded, and a true Axis invasion could well have proved victorious.

All this is important because we tend to isolate the Pacific war from the conflict in Europe and many, even American, recent histories of World War II have been somewhat Eurocentric.

As Churchill knew, only the entry of the USA could save Britain and thus democracy itself. And without the Japanese attack on Pearl Harbor the Americans would have continued to supply a beleaguered United Kingdom, but would not have been able to send the crucial supplies to the Soviet Union that were to make so decisive a difference in the USSR's fightback against the Third Reich from 1943 onwards.

Therefore, the key thing to remember is this: Japanese decisions in 1941 made *the* crucial difference to the outcome of the entire war, in Europe as well as in the Pacific. Hitler declared war on the USA on 11 December 1941, four days after Pearl Harbor. His decision enabled America to stick to its Germany First pledge to Britain. Then Japanese decisions, already taken, made all the critical difference to how the war in Europe was waged, and to its outcome. World War II really was a global war in every possible way.

One can argue that it was the same both ways around. Hitler's decision to invade the USSR in June 1941 was made without consultation with the Japanese (as had also happened with the Nazi–Soviet Pact in 1941). So confident was Hitler of a swift victory that it never occurred to him to ask the Japanese to join him. His decision strengthened the faction in Japan that favoured the southern option when the key Imperial conference took place in Tokyo on 2 July, another vital but overlooked date in World War II.

Japan's campaign of conquests begins

The goal for Japan was the Greater East Asian Co-Prosperity Sphere, a concept that dated back to 1938 but which could now be launched in earnest with attacks on the European possessions in Southeast Asia. Theoretically, this was supposed to represent Asian solidarity against white European imperialism, but in practice the human rights record of the Japanese was so barbaric – easily akin to the German treatment of Poles and other Slavic races in Europe – that in practice those who initially welcomed the Japanese as anti-colonial liberators soon regretted their joy once the countless atrocities had begun, especially against ethnic Chinese.

Thanks to the supine Vichy regime, the Japanese had already entered northern Indochina in 1940, and most of the rest of it before the invasions of December 1941 had begun. The massive oil reserves of Sumatra were essential to the Japanese war of aggression. Ships and planes needed copious amounts of oil, and both the British possessions in what is now Malaysia and the Dutch East Indies (now Indonesia) had forty-three percent of global tin production and seventy-five percent of the world's natural rubber supplies. Singapore, then as now, was one of the most important ports for international trade.

Strategically (albeit not economically), the Philippines were also vital. An attack on these islands naturally entailed war with the USA, since America still effectively ruled that country. The US Navy was increasing all the time in size, still not thinking of itself as a two-ocean force but well on the way. Many in the Imperial Navy wanted the USA crushed before such a threat could pose a problem to Japanese ambitions.

The complexities throughout the 1930s of the Japanese–US relationship is too involved to go into detail here. Suffice it to say that there was a strong pro-China lobby in the USA (partly through close missionary involvement by Americans in China since the 1840s) and Japanese aggression posed a considerable threat to US economic and strategic interests in the Pacific. America imposed sanctions on Japan, with the same lack of results that similar measures had produced after Italy's invasion of Ethiopia in 1935.

Talks led to nothing, and in October 1941 the Japanese prime minister Prince Konoe resigned, the diplomatic route becoming increasingly exhausted. The sigint breakthrough – the American discovery on how to break the Japanese diplomatic code, or MAGIC – confirmed to the USA that Japan was bent on war and destruction.

What followed was the Japanese choice that sealed their fate: the decision to use a mix of sea and air power to attack the USA, at its fleet base in Pearl Harbor, in the Hawaiian Islands. It was a sensational move, one that changed the course of the war and the world.

Pearl Harbor and the US entry into the war

Pearl Harbor, the Japanese attack on the US fleet in Hawaii on 7 December 1941 was, as President Roosevelt told the American people, a 'date that will live in infamy'. Interestingly, he did not ask Congress to declare war on Japan but to recognise that war already existed, as the result of Japanese action. The Senate agreed unanimously, the Congress having one lone maverick dissenter.

Churchill went happy to bed that night, reflecting later that 'we had won after all' – his great dream of 'the arsenal of democracy', the USA, was coming to Britain's rescue at last.

Britain may have been able to survive on its own, but could certainly never have beaten the might of Nazi Germany and imperial Japan combined. However, the involvement of the

USA was a close run thing. Had Hitler not declared war on the USA on 11 December, a vengeful USA might have prevented Roosevelt from keeping to his firm policy of 'Germany First' when the USA entered the war on Britain's side. Had he been obliged to concentrate on Japan rather than on Germany the whole war would have been radically different, and to Britain's disadvantage. Once again, Hitler's foolishness and racial attitude to the USA proved of inestimable help in the Allies' path to victory.

Here we must remember Professor Gerhard Weinberg's point in his writing on World War II, that all the different theatres of war were interlinked. This was again to the advantage of Britain and the USA, who were fully to co-ordinate all their strategic goals and plans through the various chiefs of staff and their teams in London and Washington, DC. Discussions were often stormy and disagreements frequent, but the common purpose shown by the two English-speaking Allies helped win the war.

With the other countries it would prove different. Initially, the Germans were so arrogant that they presumed that they could beat the USSR without Japanese aid, which proved to be a huge mistake. They therefore encouraged their eastern ally to go south and seize the European-ruled parts of Southeast Asia that swiftly fell as ninepins to the Japanese assault. Western racism revealed a massive underestimate of Japanese fighting prowess, Japan's victory over racially European Russian forces in 1904–05 having been swiftly forgotten.

As a result, by the time that Germany wanted the Japanese to get involved in invading the Soviet Union from the east, it was too late, especially after the naval conflict in the Pacific against the USA had turned in America's favour. Lack of Japanese/German co-operation, in comparison to that of the USA/UK, was to cost the Axis very dear.

Conspiracy theorists love to debate Pearl Harbor. There are still those who believe that what happened was the result of a subtle plot by Roosevelt or Churchill or even both of them in cahoots.

Although the Americans could read the *Magic* signals of the Japanese diplomatic corps, they did not know exactly where some of the Japanese fleet was located, nor that it was Pearl Harbor that would specifically be attacked. And not all the relevant parts of the US government spoke to each other, so that those who suspected did not get their message through to those who needed to hear it. Not only that, but few thought that the Japanese could be capable of such a long-range attack, a feeling that many in the Imperial Navy shared as well.

Indeed, apart from getting the USA into the war, and in a way that united Americans, even the isolationists, Pearl Harbor was not that successful. The three key aircraft carriers (*Lexington, Saratoga* and *Enterprise*) were not there, another major carrier, the *Yorktown* was in the Atlantic, and the ships that were sunk were old. Naval orthodoxy still averred that the key to warfare would remain battleships – the Japanese had just built the biggest such vessel in history – but as the Pacific war proved within months, it was to be aircraft carriers that would determine the outcome of the conflict.

Pearl Harbor changed the war by bringing the USA into a two-ocean war, against Japan in the Pacific and Germany in the Atlantic. As Churchill knew, only America had such power, and it was now firmly in the war and determined to prevail. Specialist historians are probably right to say that the outcome of the conflict remained in the balance until 1942–3, until after Stalingrad and the American successes in the Pacific in 1943–4.

The difference that Pearl Harbor made

After the USA entered the war it is surely accurate to say that Axis victory became impossible, and after the massive successes of the Germans in 1940–41 and the Japanese victories against the British and Dutch possessions in Southeast Asia, that is saying something. Until December 1941, the two wars (Axis vs Britain, Japan vs China) had been waged in parallel, and now, with the Japanese strike south, all of them were linked up into one genuinely global war.

Next, Pearl Harbor determined the outcome. The Japanese were massively over-extended in waging a trans-Pacific war against the USA, just as the Germans were against the USSR. Logistically, victory over the USA was a reach too far, and while for a few months it looked as if the Japanese were winning – especially against the British and Dutch empires – their success was illusory.

ROSIE THE RIVETER – AMERICAN WOMEN AND THE WAR EFFORT

Wars produce huge social change. In Britain women needed to work in the munitions factories in World War I because so many men volunteered to fight on the front line in the army. In World War II a similar need arose in the USA after 1941. So many munitions were needed that women had to break with the normal social code and enlist to become factory workers.

It was easier to recruit if potential workers had someone with whom they could identify. In 1942, the two American songwriters Redd Evans and John Jacob Loeb invented such a person: Rosie the Riveter. This fictional lady welded rivets onto the munitions that were necessary to expand the army and fight the war. She is said to have been inspired by two real-life people: Rosalind Walter who worked on the F4U Corsair, and Rose Will Monroe, who helped with the construction of the B29 and B24 bomber planes at a plant in Michigan.

Most women were not directly involved in war work during 1941–45, either in the USA or over the Atlantic in the UK. Nonetheless, in the former there were well over four million female factory workers by 1945. This in itself was a huge social change of the kind that had taken place in Britain between 1914–18. Women from now on would be very much part of the workplace, even after the war ended.

The fall of the Western empires in East Asia

The strike south was not just against the Americans at long distance but also at the British, French and Dutch empires closer to home. French Indochina was under de facto Japanese control through its rule by Vichy supporters. Britain (and many Australian troops) suffered the humiliating loss of Singapore in February 1942, with a much larger army surrendering ignominiously, after an utterly incompetent campaign, to a smaller but better-led Japanese army.

Furthermore, the demise of British rule in Malaya and Singapore, and the similar capture of the Dutch East Indies (now called Indonesia), effectively ended European rule in that part of the world, much though Churchill would have wished otherwise. The myth of white superiority, with its many racist assumptions, was shattered beyond repair, never to survive the defeats of 1942.

'Lions led by donkeys' is a term often used about the generals in France during World War I. It is seldom used in our war, but it would be highly appropriate for the leadership of the defence of Singapore in 1942, not just of General Percival, who surrendered on 15 February, but also of the unfortunately named Australian general Gordon Bennett, who fled the island.

The oft-repeated legend that the guns in Singapore were facing the wrong way (out to sea, not against an attack from the land) is sadly false. But thanks to the incompetent commanders, the defending troops were all in the wrong places. Furthermore, the Japanese forces under General Yamashita (who later became a war criminal) swept down the Malay Peninsula far faster (often by bicycle) than anyone expected. Percival failed totally to fortify the Johore area on the mainland adequately, so that the Japanese were easily able to cross the narrow straits and capture the island. No fewer than 130,000 Allied troops (a mix of British, Australian and Indian) were captured on the mainland and in Singapore by a Japanese force of less than 36,000. It is not surprising that Churchill described it as one of the worst disasters in British military history.

The maverick historian Correlli Barnett has described the fall of Singapore as the result of Churchill's decision to concentrate British forces in the struggle against Germany in the Middle East, and the new Chief of the Imperial General Staff, Sir Alan Brooke, perhaps more accurately attributed the disaster in his diary to severe imperial overstretch. Perhaps both are right – Britain could not possibly have defended itself and its East Asian possessions all at the same time. Hong Kong fell as swiftly to Japan as Singapore in a less-noticed defeat.

Feelings in Australia ran very deep on the loss – soon Japanese submarines were getting close to Darwin. Australians realised that distant Britain was not in a position any longer to defend them against a Pacific adversary. Thereafter, Australia looked to the USA for support, with MacArthur eventually establishing his base in Brisbane after July 1942 (his March 'I shall return speech' being made in Terowie, South Australia). But how could Britain have done otherwise? Victory would enable the USA to begin the fight-back against Japan.

Coral Sea and the start of the US–Japanese naval war

In May 1942, the Americans realised that the Japanese were trying to land troops in Port Moresby, in Papua New Guinea, then a colonial dependency and the natural jumping-off point for an attack on Australia. The Japanese were on a roll, and stopping them became vitally important.

The first battle was fought in the Coral Sea, around 7 to 9 May, in what one could call a draw (although the Japanese thought that they had won, which would lead them into overconfidence in the next confrontation). Both the Japanese and Americans lost ships, including the key US carrier, the *Lexington*, and each side lost substantial numbers of planes, the Japanese slightly more (105) than the Americans (81). But while neither side won, neither side lost and the invasion of Port Moresby was cancelled.

Significantly, the battle was between two fleets that could not see each other physically. This was now a carrier war, not one between traditional destroyers hitting each other within sight and at closer range. Naval warfare was changing radically and the rest of the Pacific conflict would increasingly be one in which planes (fighters, dive-bombers) were more important than the guns of ships. The USA, therefore, had succeeded in stopping the Japanese naval juggernaut's progress across the Pacific at the Coral Sea. The Battle of Midway, however, was an even more important engagement. This battle made a tremendous difference to the conflict and, as P. M. H. Bell rightly observes, enabled the USA to keep to their 'Germany First' agreement with Britain.

Midway – a victory won or a battle drawn?

The US engagement with the Japanese fleet at Midway looks more like a draw than an outright US victory. The Japanese had been furious at the American 'Doolittle' air raid on Tokyo in April 1942 (named after the US Air Force general who ordered the strike) and now in June wanted in retaliation to capture the US base on Midway (some 850 miles to the west of Pearl Harbor and midway across the Pacific). Admiral Yamamoto was a disciple of the nineteenth-century American naval strategist Admiral Thayer Mahan, whose seminal work *The Influence of Sea Power upon History* had been compulsory reading in Japanese naval circles for decades. According to Mahan's theory, a decisive victory at sea could change the course of the war and lead to certain victory, and Yamamoto wanted that victory to be his.

Unfortunately for him, on 4 June 1942, luck was against him. The initial Japanese attack was very successful, with American planes shot down. Then fortuitously a large group of US dive bombers found themselves attacking Admiral Nagumo's aircraft carriers at precisely the time when the Japanese planes were on deck and refuelling. All four Japanese carriers were sunk. The Americans also lost a carrier, but since their replacement rate was soon to be at an exponentially higher rate than Japan's, this was to give them the critical advantage in the three years ahead.

As Churchill noted in his memoirs, at 'one stroke the dominant position of Japan in the Pacific was reversed'. He was not exaggerating – P. M. H. Bell has commented that Japanese supremacy 'had been destroyed by ten bombs in ten minutes. It is hard to think of a turning point that was achieved so quickly and so decisively'.

Luck played its part at Midway. What if the US dive bombers had arrived a few minutes later and all the Japanese equivalents had not been refuelling but had been airborne? This is why American writers have referred to Midway as a miracle. That amazing timing arguably did tip the battle in favour of the USA. Or should we be more prosaic and say that Midway turned the tide in the Eastern Pacific and thus speeded up an eventually inevitable American victory that needed nothing miraculous to accomplish?

America's defensive operations: the next phase of the Pacific war

Because America held to its Germany-First commitment, offensive operations in the Pacific were ruled out until the war in

Europe permitted it. This was very controversial insofar as much of US public opinion and much of the US Navy were concerned, for whom a Japan First policy would have been preferable. However, Allied self-discipline held and no splits occurred.

But what have been called 'defensive operations' were permitted within such overall constraints. The recapture of the British-owned Solomon Islands became an American imperative, and in particular Guadalcanal, not a large island but one with strategic importance. For Admiral King, now head of the US Navy, this area was the 'tollgate' on the road to Japan, and had to be captured.

King was notoriously anti-British, a factor that looms large in many accounts of the war. He was also a Japan First supporter and resented losing that option. His strategy was, in many ways, the opposite of that argued by General Marshall about Europe. The latter strongly argued against Churchill's 'peripheral' strategy of fighting in both North Africa/Italy and directly against the enemy in northwest Europe. But in the Pacific, historians have noticed, the USA abandoned the army doctrine of hitting your main enemy directly in favour of an extraordinary strategy of fighting along what Anthony Beevor has called a 'twin axis' strategy.

Here, writers have noted, it was in essence the US armed forces arguing among themselves. Over Europe it was the US direct approach vs the British indirect or peripheral doctrine. But in the Pacific it was the US Army against the US Navy. In essence, Roosevelt solved the problem by backing *both* Pacific strategies on how best to get to Japan.

General MacArthur was put in charge of South-West Pacific Command, a land- and sea-based plan that would liberate islands such as Papua New Guinea and then continue through their region until the Philippines could be liberated. From this base the assault could take place on Japan. Then Admiral Chester Nimitz, the US Navy's Commander in Chief Pacific, was put in charge of the Pacific Ocean areas. This latter command would take a more northerly route across that ocean, with a vast and increasing naval force, and with a plan to island hop until they could meet up with the MacArthur forces for a joint invasion of enemy territory. Nimitz is sadly not well known outside the USA. He had none of MacArthur's self-aggrandising braggadocio and flair for publicity, but he was, unquestionably, one of the very greatest American commanders of the war.

Guadalcanal

The US Marines, in effect soldiers under naval command like their Royal Marine counterparts, landed easily on Guadalcanal. But the Japanese fought ferociously, and it was not until February 1943 that their remaining troops were finally evacuated.

Three key observations from Guadalcanal can be made.

First, the ferocity of Japanese fighting was to prove the same throughout the Pacific campaigns. They regarded surrender as losing honour, and so would keep going until death or the bitter end. This also raised US casualties since the Marines would effectively have to kill all the Japanese in order to win. Thus, as Michael Burleigh points out in his *Moral Combat*, American troops would be so goaded by behaviour patterns completely alien to Western psychology that this would effectively dehumanise the Japanese enemy. American soldiers would commit atrocities against them that would have been unthinkable against German or Italian troops in Europe, even though Wehrmacht troops could be as hard fighters as their Japanese allies.

Second, this was eventually to influence the most controversial Allied decision of the whole war, the atom bombs on Hiroshima and Nagasaki. We will look at these in more detail later, but suffice it to say that the American experience of trying to expel Japanese troops even from islands such as Guadalcanal led them to plan for exponentially larger US casualties when it came to thinking about capturing the Japanese main home islands in 1945. The road to Hiroshima led directly from Guadalcanal.

Third, the need to reinforce Japanese soldiers between August 1942 and February 1943 led the Imperial Navy to divert key forces and shipping away from their main US naval enemy elsewhere in the Pacific. Evan Mawdsley is surely right to argue that this was the same kind of mistake that Hitler made in splitting German forces in the southern USSR in 1942, with one group going to Stalingrad and another going after the Caucasus oil fields.

The uniqueness of American power

I would add that the critical difference is that the USA was a big enough power to fight a war on several fronts at the same time. This included a two-ocean war in both the Atlantic and the Pacific. America employed regular army troops fighting both the Germans and the Japanese simultaneously, and in the Pacific alongside the ever-growing and successful US Marine Corps. But only the USA was powerful enough to do this. Germany and Japan most certainly were not, and their division of forces in 1942 cost each of them very dear indeed, in the USSR and also in the Pacific.

In April 1943, successful code-breaking enabled the USA to assassinate Admiral Yamamoto, the Japanese thereby losing one of their best commanders. The balance of the Pacific war was now changing, and to the advantage of the USA. Japan's decision to go south in 1941 had always been a gamble. Now the results of that choice were becoming clear.

6

The Grand Alliance: The UK and USA 1941–1943

On 11 December 1941, Hitler changed the entire course of the war. It was he who declared war on the USA and not the other way around.

As we saw elsewhere, one must not overdo attributing single events as being all important and deciding the course of the whole war. But there is surely no question that Hitler's decision really did alter the war completely. Britain was now safe.

America and the Germany First doctrine

It is quite possible that Roosevelt would have been unable to persuade Congress to declare war on Hitler. US public opinion had been strongly isolationist and it was Japan's attack at Pearl Harbor that changed America's view of the war. For many Americans, Japan was the main enemy. This ran completely contrary to Roosevelt's own view and that of the US Army, particularly General George C. Marshall, Chief of Army Staff. They both preferred the Germany First option of the victory programme, the idea that the USA should come alongside Britain and defeat Germany before finishing off Japan.

Hitler's declaration enabled the US leadership to follow its own instincts and to ignore both public opinion and that of many senior officers in the US Navy, who preferred a Japan First option. The latter continued to make the defeat of Japan the main war priority and the unspoken anti-British attitude that this implied.

It is worth asking what would have happened if the USA had opted only to fight Japan. What would have happened to Britain or to the USSR? Lend-lease was helping both these two countries (and as Anthony Beevor notes, aiding the Soviet Union far more than that country ever wanted to let on). But if one looks at the history of the real war after the start of 1942, and especially after the successful Allied landings in Normandy on D-Day in June 1944, there is no question but that US active participation in Europe completely changed the nature and outcome of the war.

Churchill and Roosevelt in DC: the logistics of victory

So when a delighted Churchill arrived in Washington, DC for a three-week visit over Christmas 1941, for the first Anglo-American wartime conference (ARCADIA), he wanted to do everything possible to affirm the USA in its Germany First policy.

While much has been written about the strong disagreements between the two Allies on how to beat the Germans, we forget something rather vital upon which they agreed totally. This was their decision on 2 January 1942 massively to increase the amount of armaments that the new Allies would produce. With Britain near bankruptcy and the USA the most powerful industrial nation on the earth, this overwhelmingly meant an exponential rise in American weapons production.

Logistics do not have the excitement of battles or the drama of the significant wartime conferences. But they are the means by which war is won. (For those interested in the precise statistics, books such as Richard Overy's *Why the Allies Won* and Paul Kennedy's more recent *Engineers for Victory* make for essential reading.) The production capability of the USA was simply far greater than that of any other country. Since its factories were safe from enemy attack (we cannot really count a few stray submarines as endangering US home security) its capabilities were unaffected by war.

The only hindrance to what the USA could churn out was the U-boat threat to Atlantic shipping, and since ULTRA lost the ability to break German naval codes during much of 1942 a very large part of US military production was sunk in transit. But this was the only obstacle. All the figures show that the Germans could not produce remotely anything near US capacity – nor could the Japanese – so that the United States was uniquely able to fight both Germany and Japan at the same time, and actually to increase its own wealth in the process. The USA really was the 'arsenal of democracy' and this made all the difference in winning the war.

However, the new Allies did not agree on exact strategy, even though Britain and the USA (with the exception of some Anglophobic admirals) were united in their desire to see Germany defeated first. Much of this was due both to history and also to very different military histories between the USA and the UK. The USA was capable of being both a major land and naval power simultaneously against multiple enemies. The UK was traditionally a naval power.

However, the British were fully aware of how much they owed the USA, and what a critical difference the US support for Germany First made to Britain. Churchill, being half-American and who knew the USA well, was especially cognisant of this.

So when the Americans made what to them, and their military tradition, was the obvious suggestion about the best way to defeat Germany, the British were in a great dilemma. The USA favoured a frontal assault on German-held Europe, and as near to the actual borders of the Third Reich as possible. To Churchill, with the experience of centuries of military doctrine behind him, attacking at the periphery made far more strategic sense than the direct approach of his new American allies. However, to admit this at the beginning had the danger of playing into the hands of the Japan First lobby, including much of the US Navy. And as Roosevelt was a former assistant secretary of the navy, he was, as Churchill knew, open to unhelpful persuasion.

The forgotten meeting: Marshall and Churchill together in London

What followed in Marshall and Churchill's discussions has either been ignored altogether by historians or completely misinterpreted. However, the writer Andrew Roberts, someone familiar with the archives of George C. Marshall, has in his book *Masters and Commanders* given us the full details of what actually took place. This is significant since, in the academic debates on the role of Churchill, he is very strongly on the side of the great man and of his strategic choices.

When George Marshall and Harry Hopkins came over to Britain to follow up in early 1942 on the very productive Churchill/Roosevelt conversations in Washington they brought with them a plan that bore Marshall's name but which had in reality been composed by one of Marshall's brightest aides, a staff planner officer called Dwight Eisenhower.

We should look at this in detail because it is highly revealing of how the USA and UK were able to be close allies, yet so often disagree with each other strategically. This creative tension was in many ways a huge advantage, especially over Germany where the increasingly maniacal and deranged views of a single man determined all strategy. It was to a lesser extent helpful with the USSR, because although Stalin was eventually to agree that his commanders knew what they were doing, the very climate of fear in the Soviet Union that he created effectively precluded open and honest military debate of the kind that the Western Allies enjoyed with each other. And, as just pointed out, this is one of the most misinterpreted episodes of the war.

The codenames from the war can sometimes be complex, but what follows ought to be straightforward.

The Americans had three codenames. The first was *Bolero*, which was the massive build-up of US forces in the United Kingdom ready for whatever date in the future continental Europe would be invaded by the two new Allies. The second was *Roundup*, what we now call *Overlord*, the actual invasion of mainland Europe itself – and this, the USA recommended, would be April 1943. Then finally, since everyone was deeply worried about whether or not the USSR could withstand further battering from the Germans, there was an option for a one-off attack on Europe codenamed *Sledgehammer*, to take place in 1942, but only if the Soviets were defeated or looked close to losing.

The key thing to remember is that *Sledgehammer* was purely a contingency plan – it was emphatically not the main invasion itself, which was *Roundup*. The latter was scheduled for April 1943 and only when enough US forces had landed in the UK through the completion of *Bolero*.

Unfortunately, many historians have frequently confused *Sledgehammer* (which was very much a contingency plan only) with *Roundup*, the main plan that led to D-Day as we know it. Andrew Roberts, who has seen George Marshall's own papers, is one of the very few writers actually to understand what Marshall, Hopkins, Eisenhower and the other Americans were truly saying.

Churchill and his advisers, like the new chief of the imperial general staff Sir Alan Brooke, realised that *Sledgehammer*, if it took place in 1942, would involve almost entirely British forces. They also realised that Britain was nowhere near ready for such a frontal attack, and in any case it was completely alien to centuries of British military tradition. So they vetoed it. The Americans understood this reaction.

However, Churchill and Brooke were also totally opposed to a direct landing in Normandy or the Pas-de-Calais, not just in 1943, but almost any other year as well. For them the best way to hit the Germans was on the periphery. Since UK and British Empire troops were already in North Africa anyway, that was by far the better location for taking the war to the Germans. But if they vetoed *Roundup* as well, that would alienate their new ally and play into the hands of the Japan First group in Washington.

Few historians have actually accused Churchill and Brooke of straight lying to the Americans, and that is probably correct. But even the most sympathetic of writers has certainly admitted that the British were not entirely straight with Marshall and Hopkins, an exception to the usual cut-and-thrust honesty that marked Anglo-American relations. So when the Americans got home and found that the British did not after all agree with *Roundup* they felt entirely deceived. Marshall came as close as he was going to in the war to switching sides in the internal American debate and going after all for a pro-Japan First approach.

Most historians have looked only at *Sledgehammer* and presumed that it was 1942 that the Americans wanted for D-Day, but Marshall knew full well that this was impossible logistically. However, as a result of this confusion, the majority of writers have ignored the fact that the date that the Americans wanted was April 1943, when most of the troops scheduled to assault continental Europe would be American, not British and Canadian.

This whole debate has now become a shibboleth; nor is it a subject over which historians disagree with each other on national grounds and both the American historian Carlo D'Este, as well as the British writer Max Hastings, speak with the same voice. Churchill and Brooke were all-seeing and all-prescient, they argue, as an invasion of Europe before 1944 would have been guaranteed to be a total disaster, Marshall had no idea what he was talking about and Churchill saved the Allies from utter disaster. It is puzzling why American historians have sided with a very British perspective on that issue, but that does seem to be the case.

Torch: The Americans and British in Africa

In the end, the decision was made by Roosevelt, and for entirely political reasons. Normally he was not one to overrule his military chiefs, but he felt, with congressional elections coming up in November 1942 (and long term, the presidential race in 1944), that it was vital that Americans saw their own troops fighting the Germans at least somewhere. Waiting until April 1943 and the slow build-up implied by *Bolero* was just electorally too long into the future. So he decided to go with Churchill. The first American troops that would enter combat against the Germans would be in North Africa. This was the operation originally called *Gymnast* in the US–UK discussions, but which we now know as *Torch*. Significantly, the US commander would be the bright planning staff officer, Dwight Eisenhower.

So Churchill had won the discussion, but only in the short term. Long term Roosevelt was to side with Marshall and the US military, and insist that D-Day, while postponed from 1943, would take place in 1944 whether Churchill agreed or not.

But regardless of the debate, American troops were now engaged in the war, and in North Africa not in continental Europe. Marshall was hurt at the decision, but after threatening to side with the navy, he swallowed his pride and bided his time until the president became impatient with Churchill's peripheral approach strategy and understood that the moment for the invasion of Europe had come.

How wars are decided

One important thing is often overlooked by historians, but of which Max Hastings reminds us in *All Hell Let Loose*, his magnum opus on World War II: while the Americans in theory kept loyal to Germany First, the exigencies and sheer momentum of the war in the Pacific meant in reality that troops which were originally destined for Europe ended up in the Pacific.

In addition, Hastings' point that momentum often drove decisions applies to other parts of the war. Events have outcomes that make decisions seem inevitable at the time and create pressure for a particular direction. It is something that we can easily forget when looking back decades later, pondering why certain actions were taken. The benefit of hindsight often blinds us to pressures that built up unawares on the key leaders and carried them to making choices which, knowing what we do now, we might have made differently.

Consequently, not as many forces were allocated to North Africa, then to Italy and ultimately to northwest Europe after D-Day as the Americans originally planned. Hastings has noticed that this especially affected the USA (and therefore their Allies as well) after Normandy in 1944, when with simply more troops than he actually possessed Eisenhower could have accomplished far greater things than proved possible. Marshall was a team player, though, and accepted what the politicians had decided, whatever his own feelings.

The North African campaigns

British-based histories of World War II have given huge space to the battles in North Africa between 1940–3. From one point of view this is entirely understandable. It was mainly through fighting there that the United Kingdom was able to take the war to Germany at all. But in the overall scheme of things, the campaigns were small beer compared to the epic struggles elsewhere. While this is not to deny the considerable bravery of the troops who fought there, the whole conflict was minuscule when taken alongside the Eastern Front or the Pacific war.

Nor is it derogatory to say that Britain and the other empire forces fighting there (especially New Zealand, India and Australia) really only started to do well against the Germans when ample American supplies began to come on stream. Much equipment was needed at home in the UK, in case the Germans invaded. After the end of 1941, the wars in Southeast Asia also needed supplies.

It was excruciatingly embarrassing for Churchill to be in Washington, DC when Tobruk, near the Libyan/Egyptian border, fell to a German onslaught in 1942. But he could not have been in a better place to hear the bad news: Marshall immediately ordered the shipping of vitally needed tanks to North Africa, and it was thus a well-equipped British/Imperial force that turned the tide against the Afrika Korps later that year. We tend to forget the first Alamein battle in July 1942 as it was won under Auchinleck's command, with that old soldier being sacked by Churchill and replaced by Montgomery after the first-choice replacement General Gott's death in an accident. From November to December 1942, under the new command of General Bernard Montgomery, the Eighth Army won what should properly be called the Second Battle of Alamein. The British were unused to success and so the battle was seen as a major turning point as well as simply the defeat of Rommel's forces. It is this second battle that we usually call simply Alamein.

By the time of Montgomery's iconic victory, celebrated in Britain by the ringing of church bells, the Americans were just about to land in Morocco for *Operation Torch*, the invasion from the Atlantic coast that began on 8 November 1942.

Much British ink has been spilled over the initial US military setbacks, most notably at the Battle of Kasserine Pass where

American forces were outmatched by the Axis troops. But as the United Kingdom and its imperial allies had spent nearly two years regularly losing to Rommel, one cannot help thinking that the British are not entitled to crow. While it is arguable that Montgomery did not pursue the Germans properly after Alamein, letting many of them go to fight another day, the German menace to North Africa had effectively been removed. Although the American start had been shaky at Kasserine, some of their commanders, such as generals Dwight Eisenhower and George Patton, learned their lessons quickly and would now go on to win battles.

So much has been written elsewhere and in such detail about the North Africa war that we can pass quickly through to the Allied victory by mid-1943. Marshall had realised that with the Allies fighting in that part of the world for those crucial six months any landing in Normandy or Calais in 1943 was now out of the question.

Britain's last hurrah: the British and American ways of war

The Casablanca conference (14–23 January 1943) can be described as Britain's last hurrah as the major power on the Allied side, since the decisions taken by the British and American staff and political leaders there were, for the final time, the ones that Britain wanted.

UNCONDITIONAL SURRENDER

The Allied doctrine of unconditional surrender declared unilaterally by Roosevelt at the Casablanca conference in 1943 has turned out to be one of the most controversial decisions of the war. It has been widely blamed for stiffening Axis resistance, and for encouraging the Germans to fight on to the bitter end. Had the doctrine not existed, critics argue, then for example, the July 1944 plotters against Hitler could have tried to surrender both *conditionally* and to the West only.

Unconditional surrender meant that the Allies would not repeat their mistake of 1918 with Germany and allow the Germans to surrender on the basis of agreed terms. Germany had to surrender totally and unconditionally and be seen to be defeated.

Further, in reality, given the nature of the Nazi regime, and the fact that the July plot failed as much for lack of internal support as external factors, the idea of a conditional surrender for a regime as barbaric as the Third Reich was surely unthinkable. And since the July plotters wanted to keep many of the Hitler-conquered territories for their new regime, their terms would have in any case been unacceptable to the Allies.

Unconditional surrender also prevented Stalin from being tempted to make a deal with Hitler (which he contemplated at some of the worst moments in the war) since he knew that the Western Allies were going to fight the Germans to the very end. And it also meant that Germany was unquestionably destroyed in 1945 – no one could argue for a 'stab in the back' as in 1918. When the Third Reich was conquered by May 1945 its demise was undisputed and unquestionable.

In effect, in agreeing to preserve the emperor system, the Allies did agree to a conditional surrender with the Japanese in 1945, so they were able, in reality, to jettison their own doctrine to save the lives of millions of Allied servicemen who would otherwise have died in capturing the Japanese main island.

The decision to continue the war against Italy meant that the British position, of the indirect approach rather than head-on clash with the main enemy, was the one that prevailed. The final defeat of Axis forces in North Africa, while inevitable, was still a few months into the future. But the key decision – to liberate Sicily and then perhaps Italy – rather than to launch the main invasion of France, vindicated Churchill, Brooke and all the proponents of the peripheral approach.

This infuriated many of the American military leaders – the architect of the victory plan, General Wedemeyer, no fan of the

British, was especially incensed. For as Marshall acutely realised, Allied troops needing to take Sicily and parts of Italy completely ruled out any remote hope of D-Day taking place in 1943. What he felt was that needless British diversionary tactics, linked also to the United Kingdom's imperial interests, had prevailed against his wishes.

The Italian debacle

The Italian campaign of 1943–5 was, in the eyes of Marshall and other key American leaders, a diversion from the main campaign against Germany. And most historians would now concur with such sentiment, in that while it did tie down several German divisions – that was Churchill's great thesis and rationale – it also removed key Allied divisions from Normandy, all of whom would have been very useful to Eisenhower after D-Day.

In fact, one could argue that Churchill's best peripheral strategy was a front that never happened. He was keen on *Operation Jupiter,* which would have been Allied landings in Norway. As we saw earlier in looking at the debacle there in 1940, the main positive outcome of that military disaster was that Hitler always feared that Churchill would want to redeem himself by reinvading the country at some point. But for the wisdom of Sir Alan Brooke and later the strong feelings of the USA, Hitler would have been right since Churchill always wanted to return there.

Consequently, hundreds of thousands of German troops were sent to protect Norway from a campaign that never happened. All those forces were denied both to the German army on the Eastern Front and after 1944 to the Western Front as well. Indeed, the Wehrmacht was still there and untouched on V-E Day itself. And when they surrendered in May 1945 not a single Allied life had been lost to remove them.

By contrast, there had been some 300,000 and more Allied casualties killed and injured in the conquest of Italy (including many troops from South Africa and Brazil, as well as Polish and Free French forces). Of these roughly just under 30,000 Americans died and slightly fewer than 90,000 British soldiers were killed. (Finding exact figures for the Italian campaign is hard as sources disagree.) The German casualties appear somewhat similar albeit slightly higher.

There were many exciting tales from the war in Italy. The Battle of Anzio was one of the hardest fought during the entire conflict, as was the arduous struggle to capture Monte Cassino. But Italy was made for defenders, not aggressors, and it was only in the painfully slow progress up the peninsula that Western troops saw anything approaching the horror of Flanders in World War I.

Was the terrible Allied loss of life worth it? Would the kind of holding operation envisaged by the Americans have been better? Churchill's great hope, of breaking through the Alpine passes in northern Italy and liberating Austria ahead of the Russians, came nowhere near to fulfilment. (In 1955, the USSR withdrew from their zone of Austria, so that country was not even forced into the Soviet bloc; Churchill's great anxiety thus proving needless.)

TRUTH AND DECEPTION

In 1943, the British were able, through *Operation Mincemeat*, to persuade the Germans that the main Allied attack would be either in the Balkans or in Sardinia, and not in Sicily, where the actual invasion took place. Not merely did the Germans fall for the deception but they did so again in 1944, when they convinced themselves that D-Day would be in Calais not Normandy.

Stalin, however, twice heard the truth about genuine German plans, perceived it as deceit, and ignored it, at the cost of hundreds of thousands of Soviet lives. Not only did he do this in 1941 over Barbarossa, but also in 1942. A young German officer crashed behind Soviet lines with the wholly genuine plans for Hitler's *'Case Blue'* attack plans. Stalin was so convinced of his own judgement that he ignored the evidence entirely, and when Germany launched their attack just as the captured plans indicated, the result was nearly catastrophic for the Red Army.

So the Germans fell twice for British deception and twice the Soviets rejected the truth when it was staring them in the face: an interesting contrast between the two dictatorships.

Surely the troops from places as far afield as Yorkshire and Brazil who fought so courageously in such terrible conditions would have been better off as additions to the number of Allied troops in northwest Europe? It seems hard to say but it may well be the truth.

The Battle of the Atlantic

The year 1943 is a helpful turning point in which to look at the Battle of the Atlantic, the great naval struggle between 1939 and 1945 to get vital supplies from North America, first to Britain and after 1941 also to the USSR.

World War I had seen a major British success in blockading Germany economically, and in 1939 the British hoped that this could again be the case. However, in 1940 two things changed greatly in Germany's favour: their capture of both Norway and France, which enabled U-boat submarines to be located on a much wider stretch of the Atlantic coast of Europe. With Norway this was to be balanced by the successful defection of the Norwegian merchant fleet to Britain. This greatly expanded the scope of where U-boats could roam, and after US entry into the war in December 1941, some were even able to make it as far as the American east coast.

At one stage in the war, no less than forty-four percent of Britain's material needs came across the Atlantic from mainly the USA, or sometimes Canada. The defence of the Atlantic shipping lanes was thus vital to Britain's ability to stay in the war, which is why Churchill, in May 1941, declared the Battle of the Atlantic as begun.

The German Navy came nowhere near the capability of the British Royal Navy. So far as direct navy-to-navy conflict was concerned, there was effectively no contest, bar one or two small battles. Similarly, the Luftwaffe did not have the capability of striking too far into the Atlantic itself. Although when, after June 1941, Allied convoys came to supply the Soviets via Murmansk, such ships had to come well within German range and often suffered accordingly. But while the air forces of the Allies were never fully able to close the 'air gap' – the zone beyond the reach of their planes from either Britain or Iceland – their air supremacy over the Atlantic was never truly challenged.

Indeed one historian, P. M. H. Bell, has written that by the time the Allies finally tilted the Battle of the Atlantic in their favour by May 1943, 'air power was the most important single element in the victory'. However, this was air superiority combined with Allied technical genius over the U-boats, the German submarine fleet, for it was the threat to shipping from under the sea that was to be the major threat to the Allied convoys.

Strictly speaking, the Americans entered the war in December 1941. But to all intents and purposes, so far as vital material supplies to the beleaguered British were concerned, it was effectively September 1941 when the USA joined in, with the Germans already by then launching attacks on US shipping.

The U-boats, operating often from France, 'wolf-packs' as the Allies called them, would prey upon ships, and in some cases were able to penetrate right into the convoys themselves and pick off which boats to sink. At one stage in the war, the Allies were losing as much as 500,000 tons of vital supplies a month to sinking.

The ships were by no means all navy vessels either. Britain was proud possessor of one of the biggest merchant fleets in the world. By 1939, the UK's was the largest single fleet in percentage terms. Together with that of Canada and the gigantic Norwegian merchant ships that had escaped, these three fleets combined were far bigger than anything that even the USA possessed.

Convoys had worked in World War I, but by 1939 German U-boat technology was able to overcome much of the early Allied advantage. The Germans had several 'happy months' during which it seemed that they could sink at will. Ultra intelligence was sometimes non-existent, especially when the Germans changed their codes and made them unbreakable for months at a time. It is easy to see, by 1942, why Churchill was often so despondent, since without supplies for Britain and without US troops being able to cross the Atlantic in large numbers to aid the Allied war effort, the plight of the United Kingdom could have become dire.

The convoys that suffered the most were those taking vital supplies to the USSR. Many Allied supplies came via Siberia, unhindered by the Japanese. These convoys were well within Axis range, especially as they came near to the Scandinavian coast en route to Murmansk. Hitler was always frustrated that he had never managed to capture Archangel, the vital Russian port on

WHEN ULTRA WAS NOT ALWAYS THERE TO HELP

It has been claimed by former Bletchley Park analyst, Sir Harry Hinsley, in his official history of British intelligence in World War II, that Ultra won the Allies a whole year of war. Needless to say, many historians since then have either doubled that figure or doubted if it is even true at all.

What one can say for certain, however, is that in the war at sea, Ultra made a vast difference. It was not possible to detect German communications on land lines, so finding out what the Wehrmacht was up to was not always easy. But communications both from the

German Navy and the Luftwaffe were wireless and much easier to detect.

That is of course if one was able to break the code.

During the crucial months of February to December 1942, Bletchley was unable to decode any U-boat sigint. This meant that Allied convoys were crossing the Atlantic blind. And, not so well known, for some of this period the Germans were able to break the Allied convoy codes, so the U-boats knew where the Allied ships were and Britain and the USA were ignorant of U-boat movements.

Thankfully, another U-boat was captured, which gave the code-breakers at Bletchley the updated Enigma naval codes. So after March 1943 the Allies were once again able to decode U-boat sigint, a fact that made a vast and very swift difference.

By this time, the Allies had also made more life-saving technical breakthroughs in anti-submarine-warfare (ASW). This now meant that they not only knew where the U-boats were but also how effectively to sink them. So Ultra did make a difference for the rest of the war, but in conjunction with other parts of Allied technological superiority.

It may not have saved two years of war, but one can see from this that the absence of Ultra sigint made a huge difference and when it worked was of vital importance to the Allied effort.

the Arctic Sea. The failure of the Wehrmacht and their Finnish ally to do so was to cost Germany dear as significant numbers of Western tanks and other war material successfully reached the desperate Red Army.

The worst Allied loss was in July 1942, when of the thirty-five ships in the convoy PQ17, only eleven made it through, with twenty-four ships sunk. Churchill called this 'one of the most melancholy naval episodes in the whole of the war' and for a while the PQ convoys were stopped, to Stalin's paranoid fury.

The Allied inventions that led to victory

As Paul Kennedy shows in his *Engineers for Victory*, the Allies had technological genius on their side.

One of these was radar, already in existence. But the cavity magnetron could be used on ships after 1940 and this helped greatly to detect where U-boats might be patrolling.

Then above all there was 'radio detection-finding' or DF. Submarines all had high-frequency radio transmissions (HF) and the HF/DF combination (known by the nickname 'huff-duff') was brilliant at finding submarines. When a U-boat signalled they had found a convoy, that sigint could be picked up by Allied HF/DF and used to sink the U-boat instead, especially after 1942 when the Allied device could be placed on ships.

Finally, the British invented the 'Hedgehog', a depth charge that was able to destroy the U-boats that technology had enabled the Allies to find.

UNSUNG HEROES WHO HELPED TO WIN THE WAR

Many of us have heard of the maverick inventor Barnes Wallis, whose bouncing bomb helped the RAF's 617 'Dambuster' Squadron to blow the dams in the Ruhr in 1943 – one of the most exciting and famous air raids of the entire war. His and similar tales relate how non-combatant scientists and inventors could make a crucial difference to the outcome of the conflict. One of the best examples, though, is not a quirky scientist but a whole class of Allied sailor engineers, the Construction Battalions of the US Navy, known as Seabees (from their initials CB).

Their founder, Admiral Ben Moreell, deserves far more credit than he has ever been given. He was a hero whose transformative engineering achievements merit the admiration in which he is held. Moreell was appointed to look after the mundane-sounding Yard and Docks division of the navy in 1937. But in fact his appointment, and the work carried out by his engineers, shows that he played as critical a role in winning the war as better-known admirals such as Spruance in the US Navy in the Pacific or Ramsay in the Royal Navy on D-Day.

The Seabees were predominantly former civilians, drafted in to the navy for their construction and engineering skills. The average Seabee was thirty-seven, and their motto was *Construimus,*

Batuimus, 'We build. We fight'. They built hundreds of landing strips and harbours all over the Pacific, without which the Marines could not have held any of their hard-fought gains, or from which the USAAF could never have taken off to bomb Japanese ships and defences. Over 325 Seabees died in combat since they were frequently in the second wave of Marine attacks on Japanese positions. They fought in Europe too, in Normandy, helping to build the artificial harbours used by American troops landing after D-Day.

The other Allied superiority was in the limitless capacity to create novel kinds of ship. In particular, before the USA even entered the war, the American industrial magnate Henry Kaiser was able to make use of a British idea, that of a basic transport vessel, the 'Liberty ship'. While they were slow, they could be made at astonishing speed, usually in as little as forty days. By July 1943, more Allied ships were being built than sunk and this margin increased as the war progressed. As well as the Liberty ships, a faster kind of merchant fleet, the 'Victory ships', was in use by 1945, and the new ships of both kinds had proved their inestimable worth.

By April 1943, Allied losses were down to 270,000 tons – almost half the 500,000 ton monthly losses of the previous war. Then came what the Germans called Black May and the loss of forty-one Uboats. A naval historian has written, 'In the two weeks from 10 to 24 May 1943, ten convoys comprising 370 merchant ships passed through the German wolf packs, losing only six ships. Thirteen U-boats were sunk, while seven more were lost to aircraft attack as they crossed the Bay of Biscay. It was a decisive Allied victory.' As the Royal Naval commander Admiral Horton happily reflected, the 'climax of the battle has been surmounted'. The Germans were forced to withdraw many of their U-boats, and while the war in the Atlantic continued until May 1945, in terms of the battle for superiority at sea, the Allies had effectively won it two years earlier.

According to recent research, this meant that American troops and military supplies could now cross the Atlantic easily, making possible D-Day and all that happened thereafter. Had Britain been cut off, that would have been impossible. But Allied technology and logistical superiority carried the day, although victory on land, against Nazi Germany, was still a long way off.

The Americans take charge: how good were the generals?

When the Allied leaders met with the Canadians for the Quadrant Conference in May 1943, inter-Allied relations were distinctly tense. This was after the successful liberation of North Africa. Admiral King, no fan of the British and a firm supporter of a Japan First policy, was hoping that Marshall and the army would be so annoyed by British diversionary tactics and their insistence on fighting in Italy that he might get his way. But while Marshall seethed at what he felt was British duplicity, he nonetheless stuck to his script and the need to defeat Germany first. But he was able to insist both on a 1944 landing in northwest Europe (Normandy was not fully settled upon) and for seven divisions to be withdrawn in November 1943 from Italy ready for D-Day in France.

Historians disagree with each other about what now followed. In particular, many criticise the quality of military leadership. In retrospect, this can sometimes seem rather harsh. But surely Max Hastings is right to say that Field Marshal Sir Harold Alexander often lacked the 'grip' needed for effective command. Alexander's task in commanding Allied forces in Italy after 1943 was not easy, especially with prima donna generals such as Clark and Patton.

The contrast with Eisenhower, who was far firmer after June 1944 in northwest Europe, is rather stark. His British deputy, Air Chief Marshal Tedder, was to take Eisenhower's side against Montgomery's frequent insubordination.

MASTERS AND COMMANDERS

Who was the greatest general in the war? Or is that even a real question?

We all know about the famous and flamboyant – both MacArthur for the Americans and Montgomery for the British had excellent PR skills and a level of showmanship that helped both their reputation and, to be fair, the morale of the soldiers who fought under them.

But history has a way of changing reputations. Read, for example, Gordon Corrigan's *The Second World War: A Military History*, and a very different view of Montgomery emerges, one not at all flattering to Britain's wartime hero.

In addition, as we realise the sheer scale of the Eastern Front, any account of the conflict that underplays the role of the Russian Marshal Zhukov can no longer be taken seriously. Many historians now see him as the finest Allied commander of the whole war, the man who led the Red Army all the way to victory in Berlin.

Nationality plays a part as well. How many British people know of Admiral Nimitz, the heroic American naval commander in the Pacific? How familiar is Slim (now rated the best British general) to a US audience? Both of them played outstanding roles in the struggle against Japan.

Finally, we tend to think of battlefields, whether on land or sea or in the air when assessing wartime military leadership. But Andrew Roberts' book, *Masters and Commanders*, in highlighting the pivotal role of the two respective army chiefs of staff (Brooke for Britain, Marshall for the USA) is surely right to say that both men made as much if not more difference to the eventual outcome of the war than the more famous commanders in the field. Without the strategic grasp and genius of either Marshall or Brooke, especially the latter's weather eye on Churchill's many eccentric ideas, the war might still have been won but at much greater cost and at far longer length.

So Zhukov, MacArthur, Nimitz and Slim are rightly heroes, but so too were the leaders behind the scenes who made their victories possible.

Although the Americans were deeply sceptical of the military merits of attacking Sicily, let alone a major campaign on the Italian mainland, nonetheless the logic and momentum of war inexorably took the Allies there next; but by now Roosevelt realised that the 'Second Front', as the attack on northwest Europe was called, must not be delayed beyond 1944. He and Marshall now spoke on this with one voice. Although Churchill was successful in persuading the USA to invade both Sicily and Italy itself, he was no longer able to postpone the reckoning – a direct assault across the English Channel – whatever his fears of a repetition of the slaughter on the Somme in 1916 that dogged British thinking on a frontal assault on the Third Reich. When US troops landed in increasing numbers in Britain, it would be in preparation for D-Day, the largest amphibious assault in history.

So much has been written about Allied bombing campaigns during World War II that to take up space here might be superfluous. However, 1943 saw a daring raid by the Royal Air Force. The Dambusters of 617 Squadron have gone down in history and can be regarded as symbolic of the RAF area bombing of Germany

The May 1943 raid against the major German dams (principally the Eder and the Moehne) by a specially formed 617 Bomber Squadron of the Royal Air Force became one of the legendary raids by Bomber Command. Guy Gibson, the plucky commander, was given the Victoria Cross and the aircrew who survived (forty-two percent did not) became popular heroes. Their fame increased when a film was made in the 1950s that, combined with its film score, turned war heroes into legends.

The story also had the archetypal eccentric boffin, Barnes Wallis, whose invention of a bouncing bomb that could destroy the outer walls of the dams, became symbolic of Churchill's full backing for the weird and wonderful in the scientific community. Some of these ideas were impractical and crackpot, but others, like the bouncing bombs, turned out to be genuine winners that in some cases, such as the artificial Mulberry harbours built on the Normandy beaches after D-Day in 1944, helped to shorten the war and save Allied lives.

Needless to say, revisionists were soon downplaying the importance of the raids. It is true that the dams were rebuilt and that as well as nearly half the air crew losing their lives so too did thousands of civilians living in the path of the water pouring out of the broken dams. New research, however, has shown that the dislocation to the economy of the Third Reich was massive – tens of thousands of tonnes of coal and steel production was lost – and that those who had to rebuild the dams would otherwise have been employed in reinforcing the Atlantic Wall, the defences against which the Allies had to fight in Normandy after D-Day.

Deeds of valour have been of great morale-boosting value since time immemorial and the Dambuster raid certainly provided plenty of that to a battered British public. The fact that Barnes Wallis' idea was implemented is symbolic of Churchill's appreciation of the oddball, and although the cost was as high as the critics suggest, one can go too far in criticising the heroes of the past. The Dambuster raid, however flawed, surely still deserves its legendary status.

The media portrayal of the war

The 1955 film version of the Dambuster raid does make for a brief but relevant discussion on how the war was portrayed in its aftermath.

But in fact how much of what we think happened during the war is influenced by Hollywood and by similar British film portrayals of the conflict? How distorted is our image?

Sometimes films that portray the war are not too distant from what actually happened. *A Bridge Too Far* does not cover up the fact that *Market Garden*, the attempted capture of the Rhine crossings, ended up as a complete mess, including the fiasco of the failure to seize the bridge at Arnhem – the 'bridge too far'. Likewise veterans all agree that the American TV series *Band of*

Brothers really is an excellent portrayal of what it was like to be in such a regiment in Western Europe from 1944–5. Also the British film *Ill Met By Moonlight,* about the successful SOE capture of a German general in Crete, is also based entirely on truth.

But it is not that simple.

First of all, even films that have been highly praised, such as *Saving Private Ryan*, can be accidentally misleading. How many British or Canadian soldiers do you see in it? Or for that matter in *Band of Brothers*? Yet while American troops predominated in northwest Europe after D-Day, the invasion was very much an Allied effort from start to finish. Hollywood distorts this, for commercially understandable reasons, but it does not give a wholly balanced portrayal as a result.

Even more important is one of the key statistics of this book: eighty-five percent of the Wehrmacht fought on the Eastern Front. A film such as *Enemy at the Gates* goes in a small way to remind us of this but, by and large, it is easily possible to think that the Western Allies won the war against Germany without any reference to the Soviets.

The big three: Stalin joins in the discussion

The direction of the war was now going firmly in the way that the Americans wanted and now they were to have Stalin on their side.

The Tehran Conference ('Eureka' of 28 November to 1 December 1943) was one of the most important in the war. Yet coverage of it seems patchy – serious histories either gloss over it briefly or dedicate whole chapters to it and declare it to be one of the pivotal moments in the war.

The gathering was a turning point for Churchill when he realised that Britain was no longer a player in the same league as the USSR, certainly so far as the USA and President Roosevelt were concerned. In public huge coverage was made of the fact that this was the first time that the big Three (Churchill, Roosevelt and Stalin) had all met together, though, as the British were to rue, it was in reality the big two-and-a-half, the two future superpowers, as we would now see it, with the once great United Kingdom.

In Tehran in 1943, Winston Churchill later confessed to his old friend Lady Violet Bonham-Carter that he felt he, the poor little British donkey, was being squashed between the American buffalo and the Soviet bear, even though it was only the rather flattened donkey who knew the way home.

The popular American as well as British perception of Churchill is as a roaring bulldog, not a squeezed-upon donkey, so his was a strange analogy. But it does demonstrate very vividly how much the internal balance of power between the three wartime leaders had changed by 1943, and not at all to Britain's advantage. Roosevelt was ostentatiously ganging up with Stalin to show the Soviet dictator that there was no collusion among the Western democracies against the USSR. Churchill found this rather hurtful.

In the hindsight brought to us by the Cold War, Roosevelt was being perhaps rather naive if not foolish. But given the exigencies of the time, combined with Roosevelt's natural distrust of Britain as an old-fashioned imperialist power, one can see what the president was trying to achieve. By 1943, the USA had emerged as the indispensable global power, with the United Kingdom all but bankrupted by four years of war. FDR might have been an insensitive buffalo, but the nature of global power had decisively shifted from the Old World to the New.

In terms of significance, one could say that Tehran therefore embodied the power shift. It was a time of recognition, a confirmation of how the war had already been going and how the war was now going to proceed until the Nazis were soundly beaten.

First, despite Churchill's zealous defence of Britain's traditional peripheral strategy and his desire to see even more Allied troops sent to fight in Italy, the Americans were now able to get together with the Russians and insist that *Overlord*, the landing of massive Allied armies in northwest Europe, could no longer be postponed. It was scheduled for May 1944 whether Churchill liked it or not. Britain was no longer in a position to call the shots or to veto what the USA wanted to do.

The Americans now made it clear that their direct approach way of waging war was non-negotiable. No one had yet been appointed to command this huge enterprise – to Stalin's amazement – but while the obvious candidate for the job was Marshall, Roosevelt wanted the great organiser of war close by in Washington, DC, so the task went to Eisenhower instead.

Second, by the time of the Tehran conference, the Soviets had brought to an end the siege of Stalingrad and won the battle of Kursk. The Red Army juggernaut was now inexorably moving westwards. By November 1943, there could be no doubt as to its eventual destination and victory.

With no Western troops fighting the Germans in France, Britain and the USA were thus in a very weak negotiating position in relation to Stalin. They had no choice but to accede to the Soviet dictator's demands for territorial gains at the expense of those countries his armies were now about to conquer.

A good war no more? The democracies and Stalin at Tehran

One can therefore say that Tehran meant that the West was no longer fighting a 'good war'. We were of course fighting the Nazis in Europe and the Japanese in Asia, both of which were morally wholly commendable things to do. But now the price of the fact that our main ally against Nazi Germany was the equally despotic USSR was becoming apparent. Stalin had ruthlessly conquered eastern Poland in 1939, killing or exiling hundreds of thousands of innocent Poles, and then in 1940 he had simply extinguished the independence of the three Baltic States (Estonia, Latvia and Lithuania). And all this had been in alliance with Hitler.

Now he insisted on keeping all his gains from the days of the Nazi–Soviet Pact. And with the Red Army about to 'liberate' these countries and the armies of the Western democracies nowhere near Germany, there was, in reality, not much that Churchill or Roosevelt could do, whether they wanted to or not. And while Churchill now became worried about the fate of Poland, even as late as 1945, he was still thinking that he could do business with Stalin, such as in his speech to the House of Commons upon his return from Yalta early that year. So despite legend to the contrary, when it came to the Soviet dictator, he was every bit as deluded as Roosevelt.

Therefore, Tehran exposed three things:

1) America and the USSR were the nations that counted and Britain was relegated to the second division.
2) D-Day would happen in 1944, and British rights of veto on American policy were now over.
3) Although Britain had gone to war in 1939 to defend Poland, the reality of troops on the ground meant that a betrayal of the Poles to the Soviets was inevitable, however uneasy the Western democracies might feel.

After Tehran, Churchill fell dangerously ill with pneumonia. He narrowly escaped death and decided to recuperate in Tunisia, where he recovered fully in the warm sunshine. But his days as a major war leader were now effectively over. Henceforth, all the plans that he came up with (a Third Front in Norway or in the upper Adriatic near Ljubljana) were now firmly squashed by the Americans. He might feel he was the donkey who knew the way but with American power building up ready for D-Day, there was no doubt as to who was in charge.

7
The Path to Berlin 1944–1945

D-Day at last

D-Day, 6 June 1944, was the day that the Second Front finally began in Europe. It was the liberation of Europe from the West. The Americans could now wage war their way, against the main enemy Germany and against the territory of the Third Reich itself.

And while thousands died on the Normandy beaches, it was not remotely near the carnage that had been expected by both Winston Churchill and by his chief of the Imperial general staff Sir Alan Brooke. This was no first day of the Somme. The ghosts of the earlier conflict were now finally exorcised as the Allies not only captured the landing beaches but established permanent footholds in northwest Europe.

Eisenhower famously had a slip of paper ready with an apology that put all the responsibility upon him in case the landings proved to be an utter disaster. But it was not needed. All the planning and all the immense courage of the thousands of soldiers proved worthy of the effort that had gone into making the day one that would go down in history as a success.

Some historians, such as Anthony Beevor, who has written about D-Day in enthralling depth, still argue that it could all have gone wrong, that the weather that delayed it for a day could have done so for weeks, and that to use an analogy from another British victory, that of Waterloo in 1815, it was a close run thing.

OPTIMISTS VS PESSIMISTS

D-Day, the Western Allied invasion of the Normandy beaches, took place on 6 June 1944.

But if the British had had their way, it might never have taken place at all. As late as the night before, Churchill feared that twenty thousand young soldiers would die attempting to land, and the deep pessimism of his chief of the Imperial general staff Sir Alan Brooke was not much different – he too feared another Battle of the Somme, with nearly sixty thousand British casualties on the first day.

D-Day was, as Anthony Beevor reminded *BBC History* readers in 2013, far from guaranteed. The storm that created such havoc a few weeks later could have coincided with the invasion and, as it was, Eisenhower had to postpone the original planned landing day because of the weather. But could the sheer logistical might of the USA have been defeated long-term by the Third Reich?

Pessimism – with understandable historical roots in the Great War experience – seems built into the British DNA. What is surprising is that even American historians seem to have caught the bug, despite what would seem to be overwhelming evidence to the contrary. Just look at how well American troops fared in both northwest Europe against the Germans and in the Pacific against the Japanese. The Canadians, New Zealanders and Australians all fought with distinction. Most Western soldiers were civilians in uniform and deserve the fullest credit for their unstinting service.

One does wonder whether this is traditional British pessimism at work. Now that the overwhelming might of the USA was fully engaged, it is hard to see how the Allies could have lost. Individual battles were certainly lost, and the route to Germany and beyond took much longer than the British, Americans and Canadians anticipated. There was to be no victory in 1944.

Some D-Day myths

There are myths about D-Day that do need revision. The first is that once the Western Allies had landed, the war was won. In fact, as we see elsewhere in this book, there were contemporaneous battles on the Eastern Front massively larger than anything on D-Day. One example is *Operation Bagration* which dwarfed anything that happened on the Normandy beaches. (*Bagration*, from June to October 1944, swept the Germans out of what is now Belarus and eastern Poland. Well over two million Red Army troops were involved, significantly higher than Allied forces in Normandy.)

What one can say about D-Day is that its success ensured that Western Europe would be liberated by the forces of the democratic powers. Success also meant that those nations freed by the USA, Britain and Canada would themselves therefore be democracies once the war was over. At the same time, one of the greatest tragedies of World War II was that millions of Central and Eastern Europeans were saved from one dictatorship only to fall under the domination of another for over forty years. However, D-Day was a major achievement and worth the sacrifice of all who died to ensure it. In the long term, it was NATO that guarded the safety of West European countries, but it was the victory on D-Day that made such a configuration possible.

The second myth is the idea that the troops of Western Allies were simply no good at fighting and that their leaders were not up to par with those of the Third Reich. It is arguably true that the Allies took much longer to break out of Normandy than they had planned, and that countless Germans who should have been captured escaped encirclement. Vast amounts of ink have been spilled on this. The supposedly slow pace after D-Day is beloved of 'armchair generals' and few episodes in the war have been more refought than this one.

In particular, the fact that Field Marshal Montgomery, the land commander (until Eisenhower assumed total command), insisted that absolutely everything that happened had gone according to his plans – including the delays in capturing Caen, for instance – has provoked many writers into rethinking his place in the

Olympus of truly great British generals. Now, though, he has his defenders: John Buckley's *Monty's Men: The British Army and the Liberation of Europe* suggests that British troops were better than recent historians have given them credit. And is it a criticism to say that the British as a nation lack martial vigour? Or that they have a natural tendency to question authority? These can be good traits as well as bad.

Montgomery's excessive caution and contempt for his American Allies were certainly not helpful, and it was only his unsackable status (post-Alamein) in Britain and his protection by Churchill and Brooke that stopped Eisenhower from sacking him when his insubordination became unacceptable. Other British corps commanders were sacked in the early months and they too can be said to have lacked the grip necessary to fight the Germans.

How brave were the Americans?

But is this criticism also applicable to the Americans, who are also a democracy? The US commanders were made of victory-winning material, and the bravery of the 'Greatest Generation' GIs is surely incontestable. It is a shame that many American writers have bought into the British denigration of Allied prowess and have preferred the caution of a Montgomery to the greater wisdom of a Bradley or Patton.

And finally, while both British and American commanders were casualty-averse, this high regard for human life is surely one of the values for which the West was fighting. It may have resulted in a slower rate of victory against the Germans, but would the democracies really have wanted the carelessness towards massive casualties that pervaded the Soviet and German leadership? One would hope not.

The breakout from Normandy and beyond

So minute is the detail in which the next few months of the war have been analysed and dissected that there is no need to do so here. The battles in Normandy had to be fought in geographically unhelpful territory. Large hedgerows, called *bocage* in French, slowed up the advance considerably, and the timetable had to change accordingly. But on 1 August, Patton was given active command, and the war was able to begin in earnest. While the Battle of the Falaise Gap was no Kursk, some 50,000 Germans were killed and 200,000 captured (with 300,000 escaping to fight the Allies another day).

Simultaneously, *Operation Anvil* began on the south coast of France, on 15 August. Eighty thousand Allied troops landed and by mid-September the forces coming in from this direction had linked up successfully with those coming from Normandy.

The French now had some good news. It was important to French national pride for their own troops to capture Paris, which fell to Free French forces on 25 August. The next day General de Gaulle was able to walk in victory down the Champs Elysees. But following liberation the French had to confront the fact that many of them had not only collaborated with the Nazi or Vichy authorities but had done so willingly.

France has had a long internal debate over the years 1940–5 ever since. Collaboration with the Vichy regime or with the Nazis may have made for a peaceful life at the time, but after the liberation in 1944 such activity was seen in a sinister light. For many French people, these years soon became best forgotten. The genuine extent of collaboration and resistance remains murky.

As 1944 progressed, the Allies began to face the same logistical problems that had dogged the Wehrmacht in the USSR – supply lines that were far too long. Not as many ports had been captured as there should have been, and so the vital supplies needed for a victorious army were increasingly bottlenecked. Even Patton's forces could not continue without petrol for the tanks, and so much of the successful invasion force now came to a halt.

The July 1944 bomb plot

Events in France did not go unnoticed in Germany especially among those elements in the opposition to Hitler who wanted an excuse to get rid of him.

After 1945, it became vital for German self-esteem to find 'good Germans' who had genuinely been anti-Hitler. The anti-Hitler military and political plotters in July 1944, now made famous in the Hollywood treatment of their action in *Valkyrie*, have provided the best example. They tried to get rid of Hitler by blowing him up, and in July 1944 they almost succeeded. The plotters have historical importance in the discussion on unconditional surrender, since they would have wanted to deal with the Western Allies but not with the Soviets.

Bold though the plot leaders undoubtedly were, there was a fundamental flaw in their objective. They were certainly no modern democrats and they wished to keep hold of large swathes of German conquests. Their terms would therefore have been as unacceptable to the British and Americans as they would most certainly have been to Stalin. And if the West had made peace with a group of what we have to describe as well-meaning reactionaries, would the USSR have agreed to end the war on such terms? One rather thinks not.

It is unlikely, even if they had succeeded in killing Hitler, that the plotters would have been able to persuade the bulk of the Wehrmacht to go with them. One cannot imagine what the substantially well-armed SS divisions of the armed forces might have done to alter a coup. A civil war within Germany would have.

Unlike 1918 when to many Germans the war ended with a treacherous 'stab in the back', there was no question in 1945 that the Nazis and the German state with them had been unquestionably and utterly defeated. This was surely a better and more conclusive end to the fighting than a dubious peace with non-Nazi but essentially reactionary German nationalists. The sheer nerve of the plotters is highly commendable and they died as martyrs, but it was as well for the long-term future peace of Europe that their plot failed and that the Allies – including the USSR – kept to unconditional surrender.

The bridge too far

Montgomery's appointment as land commander in north-west Europe in June for D-Day was not intended to last the entire campaign against Germany. He was now appointed as commander of the 21st Army Group, under the overall leadership of Eisenhower as executive supreme Allied commander. This change took place on 1 September. But Montgomery still hankered for control of the overall direction of the war.

Having been far too cautious throughout his military career, Montgomery therefore decided on a highly rash and daring move, to follow upon the successful Allied liberation of France. He wanted to be able to cross the Rhine and enter the Ruhr – the industrial heartland of the Third Reich itself – and thus across the North German Plain and on to Berlin. This was *Operation Market Garden*, a plan to seize the Rhine bridges so that troops could then cross from the Netherlands into Germany. To do this involved parachute drops of thousands of paratroopers, who would capture the bridges until the main armies could catch up with them and secure the entry into the Third Reich. Some thirty thousand airborne troops – British, American and Polish – would take part.

As we now know, the whole episode was to end in disaster – in fact it is mainly famous through the book and film that shows this: *A Bridge Too Far*. (The film itself leaves out Montgomery, who died just before it was released.) Some of the bridges were captured with ease but although the Arnhem bridge across the Rhine was captured by intrepid British Parachute Regiment forces, the main troops were not able to get that far (hence the title) and the paratroopers had to surrender. Some 2,000 British and Polish paratroopers managed to escape, but over 2,500 were killed and 4,500 captured.

Market Garden has been recorded as a disaster. Montgomery has rightly been criticised for it, and it is quite probable that Arnhem was indeed a 'bridge too far'. However, while counterfactuals can be controversial or sometimes facile, historian Mitchell Bard does have an excellent point when he writes:

> If Operation Market Garden had succeeded, the Allies would probably have reached Berlin before the Russians, ending the war by Christmas 1944, saved thousands of civilian and military lives and perhaps changed the fate of postwar Europe. Instead, it took another four months before the Allies crossed the Rhine and began the final conquest of Germany.

The final sentence is irrefutable. There are of course a lot of 'ifs' in the rest of what he says, and a Christmas victory might still have been unrealistic. But it does suggest what could have happened if Montgomery's rare flash of bravery had come to pass, and also if he had tried to be more audacious sooner.

Hitler's last throw: the Battle of the Bulge

After *Operation Market Garden* there was a major period of standstill in the West, broken only on 16 December 1944 when Hitler tried his very last gamble to prevent the Allies from landing upon German soil.

Hitler had been planning this operation for some time, to the despair of many of his commanders, who knew that troops were urgently needed on the Eastern Front. He was determined to attack in the West, hoping against all the odds that he could cut the Allies off and achieve in 1944 what he had done in very different circumstances in 1940.

When the attack came the Allies were caught completely off guard. The area in the Ardennes where the SS panzer divisions launched their offensive was as unmanned in 1944 as in 1940. Worse still, the American First Army commander General Hodges was cut off. Temporary command of many US forces had to be conceded by Eisenhower to Montgomery, who proceeded to claim all the victories gained by the hard-fighting American troops to his own genius.

The troops under Hodges' command had also suffered horribly in the Battle of the Hurtgen Forest, the first fought by Allied soldiers on actual German soil, and in which nature gave a huge advantage to the defenders over the invaders.

The German thrust created a huge bulge in the Allied lines (hence the name). But thankfully the Germans were short of precious fuel – an attempt by SS leader Otto Skorzeny to create a group disguised as Americans to capture vital supply dumps did not succeed. In addition, Patton was able to turn his troops around some ninety degrees and launch a successful counter-attack: although his vanity that he could do so with just three divisions elongated the battle since that number was inadequate to deal with the Germans, even for him.

As Beevor is right to argue, the Battle of the Bulge saw Eisenhower at his very finest, able to respond rapidly to the unexpected attack, co-ordinate Allied response and defeat the Germans decisively.

The American defence of Bastogne is one of the finest moments in US military history, made legendary by their commander General McCauliffe's response to the Germans who

asked him to surrender: 'Nuts!' The incredible heroism in particular of the airborne divisions, forced to fight from trenches and
fox-holes, shows that US soldiers were the equal of their German
opponents any time. And there was also the gruesome danger of
wild bears in the forest eating unwary humans – it is not surprising, as Beevor reminds us in making use of his experience as an
officer in the British Army, that the psychological state of many
of the forces hung by the narrowest of threads.

While the Americans lost thousands who were injured or
captured, they had nonetheless survived. The Germans meanwhile had lost well over ninety thousand killed, injured or
captured – and well over six hundred tanks, many of which had
simply run out of fuel. Hitler's great Western gamble had failed,
and the road to Germany now lay open.

The Western Allies contemplate their next move

The Allied advantage remained considerable once the Battle of
the Bulge was over. The Germans could not replace their losses,
but tens of thousands of new American troops were now landing
in Europe, ready to engage and finish off the Nazi foe.

In other places, the Germans were losing too, especially on the
Eastern Front. In October 1944, they withdrew from Greece, and
their days in the Balkans were numbered. The British decision to
send troops to Greece was controversial because Churchill was
taking sides in a civil war between the Royalists (who wanted
the return of the king, a relative of the British royal family) and
the Communists. In Greece, however, Stalin had kept his word to
Churchill and did not intervene to help his fellow Communists,
who thereupon lost the civil war.

Endless debate has taken place on what happened next
as the Western Allies now prepared to invade Germany itself.

CHURCHILL'S NAUGHTY DOCUMENT

In late 1944, Churchill visited Stalin in Moscow to discuss the progress of the war. When there he signed a spheres of influence deal with Stalin – his so-called 'naughty document' or the 'percentages agreement'.

In essence, the two leaders carved up Eastern Europe in terms of which country would have the predominant influence once the war was over. Greece, whose royal family Churchill strongly supported, would be in the Western zone under British sway. Yugoslavia, whose Communist partisans had been supported by Britain since 1943 (the Enigma decrypts showed that Tito's partisans were fighting the Germans better than the royalist Cetniks) would be 50:50. Countries such as Bulgaria and Romania would be predominantly under Soviet control. Originally, Hungary was also to be 50:50, but tragically for that country Molotov was able to persuade Eden, the British foreign secretary, to make Hungary more under the Soviets than under Britain.

These discussions were done without any consultation with America at all. The USA was justly furious. It was a piece of cynical realpolitik and condemned millions of people to Soviet tutelage.

However, three things need to be said.

Thankfully, once the war really was over, the new American president, Harry Truman, decided to keep US troops in Europe rather than to send them home or to fight Japan. Churchill did not know this in 1944 since Roosevelt intended to remove American forces after the war as Woodrow Wilson had done in 1919. No one was even dreaming of NATO in 1944.

Second, Stalin kept his word. He did not intervene in the Greek Civil War that began shortly after Churchill's visit to Moscow, and so the Greek Communists lost. And in 1948 when Tito declared Yugoslavia to be a country that was still Communist but no longer in the Soviet bloc, the USSR did not invade, unlike with Hungary in 1956.

Third, historians have noticed that there is no mention of some other key European countries. (The fate of Poland was always discussed between the three major Allies, with full American involvement.) Czechoslovakia fell under Communist rule in 1948, but Italy, despite having a large Communist party, did not, and nor did France, to which the same applied. Churchill was not able to get American troops to liberate Prague, but he was able to make sure that Montgomery's forces got to the key parts of Germany in 1945 which prevented a Soviet incursion into Denmark. And Stalin kept to the zones agreed by all three major allies in Germany.

So perhaps the naughty agreement, while unwise, was justified in the circumstances after all.

Montgomery wanted a bold thrust to the north, whereas Eisenhower preferred a wider front. In the short term, Eisenhower gave some of Bradley's divisions to Montgomery's command; in the longer term, some of those forces would return to American leadership. And the battle as to which commander was correct has waged fiercely ever since!

The Yalta Conference and the fate of Poland

The Yalta Conference took place in Ukraine at the former resort town in the Crimean peninsula, an area that had only recently been liberated from the Germans. The three major leaders – Stalin, Roosevelt and Churchill – gathered there in early February 1945. Their deliberations have become infamous for the supposed surrender of Poland to Stalin and for the tragic decision to allow Soviet prisoners of war to be sent home to the USSR, where thousands were shot by the NKVD on arrival.

On the Polish issue, it is arguable that that country's fate had already been sealed in Russia's favour by the Western Allies, both at Tehran and by the decisions made by Churchill and others to recognise the borders gained by Stalin in 1939–40, during the era of the Nazi–Soviet pact. At Yalta itself, Churchill was deeply concerned by what he saw as Stalin's wish to swallow up large swathes of Polish territory, and by the latter's rather evident plans to install a puppet pro-Soviet government in Warsaw, whether the Polish people actually wanted Communist rule or not. But by now it was far too late, since Red Army troops controlled the territory of both pre- and post-1939 Poland, and had no intention of leaving.

Furthermore, the savagery of the Soviet decision in 1944 to let the Polish Home Army be destroyed in the latter's uprising against the Nazis in Warsaw from August to October 1944 demonstrated very clearly what Stalin's intentions were. Anything that the West might have liked to do at Yalta was now physically impossible, short of launching a third world war against the USSR to liberate Poland from its new occupiers.

One can therefore argue that Yalta was the culmination of a long process of betrayal of Polish interests by the West rather than the occasion of it. In Britain's case, while the United Kingdom had entered the war in September 1939 to protect Poland, it was very clear then that there was nothing that the British could actually do, especially since the Nazi–Soviet pact in effect meant that the country was attacked from both sides by the two dictator nations. The problem of how to get effective practical aid over long distances to help the Poles was the same in February 1945 as it had been in September 1939. The fact that it had proved impossible for Western aid to get to the Warsaw Uprising in 1944 because of Soviet intransigence only reinforces this point.

None of this diminishes the tragic fate that befell Poland, and the fact that over four decades of foreign oppression would follow. Churchill, with the Polish sorrow in mind, deliberately named his sixth and final volume of the history of the war as *Triumph and Tragedy*.

Few people knew about the other tragic decision taken at Yalta until 1977, when a British member of the Tolstoy family wrote a book entitled *The Victims of Yalta*. This demonstrated that thousands of Soviet prisoners of war found by the Western Allies were forcefully sent back to the Soviet Union.

The British also repatriated Russians who had left the USSR during or soon after the Russian revolutions of 1917, and who were therefore theoretically not Soviet citizens. Women and children were also compulsorily sent home and many of the former committed suicide on the train journey, which distressed the British soldiers obliged to send them.

The secret had in fact been revealed by Nicholas Bethell's book *The Last Secret* in 1974, but Tolstoy's surname and the court case for libel that was associated with him made the case infamous. The British were very worried about getting their own prisoners of war back from German prison camps liberated by Red Army soldiers, and in 1945 the USSR was still thought of as a key wartime ally, as opposed to the Cold War enemy that it would later become. (And this continues to dog all issues in relation to Stalin and the USSR: we see everything in hindsight through the prism of the Cold War decades and forget how people would have seen it at that time, without such knowledge.)

Perhaps with the repatriations we can now say that they were an accidental tragedy, the result of what seemed to the Allied leaders at Yalta to be an easy decision, but which on the ground was a calamity leading to immense suffering.

Both the agreements on Poland and on the repatriations all led to the same thing: Stalin was the winner and it was his Red Army forces steamrolling across Central Europe that was the major military factor on the ground. While the decision of the Western Allies to postpone D-Day from 1943 to 1944 is now something so inbuilt into the canon that it cannot be contradicted, the inevitable result of that postponement, even if totally justified on military grounds, meant that much of Europe was conquered by Soviet troops from Nazi control rather than being liberated for democracy by the Western Allies.

The price of D-Day being a guaranteed success in 1944 as opposed to a probable catastrophe in 1943, as believed totally by the keepers of the most widely held version, is that thousands of British and American lives were thereby saved. However, one can argue that this was at the expense of millions of people in Central and Eastern Europe suffering for over four decades under Soviet rule. Yalta was a tragedy but it could not have been otherwise.

The fight for Germany begins

Fighting on the Siegfried Line of German defence began in earnest by February 1945, with the breakthrough occurring in March. Then the Allies had a lucky break – the American First Army found a bridge across the Rhine at the town of Rema-gen that was still just about intact. The Americans were able to sweep over and into Germany, and then Patton's troops achieved a breakthrough, wiping out the remnants of German resistance in the process.

Meanwhile, as the Western Allies were poised on the edge of the Third Reich itself, the three major leaders decided that it was time to meet again.

With Patton's forces in Germany proper by 22 March, the decision time had come for where to go next. So the next day Montgomery's forces launched *Operation Plunder*, the massive main Allied crossing of the Rhine. And as Evan Mawdsley has pointed out, this time the parachute assault – *Operation Varsity* – was as successful as *Market Garden* was not.

So with considerable military success under their belts, the Allies now disagreed on where to go next. Montgomery wanted a direct northern thrust (similar, historians point out, to the Soviet 'deep war' strategy), whereas the Americans wanted a broader thrust, both north and south.

Much of this dispute relates to the issue of the race to capture Berlin. While Bradley apparently later felt that his advice to Eisen-hower that for the Allies to assault Berlin would take 100,000 lives was perhaps exaggerated, the fact that it took two Soviet armies joined with some Polish regiments and 75,000 deaths to capture the German capital rather suggests that Bradley's figure was close to the mark.

100,000 DEATHS FOR BERLIN

One of the most controversial decisions at the end of the war was that of Eisenhower, in keeping to the Tehran agreements confirmed at Yalta that the Soviets would capture Berlin, and that the Western Allies would respect the prearranged zones of occupation. To Churchill's fury, he confirmed this in a telegram from Allied Headquarters (SHAPE) to Stalin, and with consultation only with his superiors in Washington, DC – Churchill was left out of the loop.

But what actual difference would it have made if the Americans had captured Berlin instead of the Red Army? Surely Berlin was now in effect a purely political objective not a military one. That was certainly the view of the Americans, and of both Eisenhower and his military superior, General George C. Marshall. If 100,000 lives were to be lost, better that they were Soviet than American.

Some historians such as Chester Wilmot, in his highly influential book *The Struggle for Europe*, have supported Churchill and Field Marshal Montgomery, who would have loved to have been the conqueror of Berlin. But this is, in reality, to read the subsequent history of the Cold War back into 1945. The Red Army juggernaut was closer to Berlin and Stalin was more than happy to pay the blood price to capture the German capital, in a way that the Western Allies, who had far more regard for human life, were not.

The Berlin airlift of 1948–9 showed that the Western Allies were determined not to let the whole city of Berlin fall into Soviet hands, and they were to rule over most of the city throughout the Cold War. This was with the Soviets having spilled Red Army blood in 1945. So would 100,000 American troops have died in a 'race for Berlin' as some wanted? Anthony Beevor has suggested that they would have had large casualties and maybe even suffered from Soviet 'friendly fire'. Stalin was desperate to capture the German capital and might, Beevor suggests, have ordered his troops to fire as if by accident on US forces. That is hypothesis but surely Eisenhower made the right decision.

Where Eisenhower was wrong was his fear of an 'Alpine redoubt', a Wagnerian place of last German resistance centred on Bavaria in the south. No Ultra material vindicated this chimera – although Eisenhower was by no means alone in believing the redoubt to be genuine – so it proved a complete red herring. However, given the actual death toll for Berlin, and the fact that Stalin had conceded occupation zones of the city for the Western Allies, then perhaps the mythical last stand was a godsend that accidentally saved the lives of thousands of Allied troops.

As historians remind us, while taking the Rhineland cost the US Army 40,000 deaths, only 10,000 were killed between crossing the Rhine and D-Day. Allied losses in 1945 have been estimated to be less than ten percent of the 770,000 Red Army troops killed or missing in the same period.

It is thought that some 1.4 million German troops died in the same period – some thirty percent of all German casualties throughout the entire war – most of these being naturally on the Eastern Front. But between 25,000 and 40,000 civilians were slaughtered in a single night in the Allied air raid on Dresden on 13 February, whose strategic rationale is still disputed. It is important to put Dresden into context, but it was surely not necessary to overall Allied victory and those who consider it a blot on the record of the Allies are surely right to do so.

Berlin endgame and the death of Roosevelt

President Roosevelt died on holiday on 12 April 1945. Goebbels, remembering a previous war in which the death of the Russian tsarina saved Prussia, hoped that it would save Germany. Thankfully he was utterly wrong. President Truman might not have been experienced in foreign policy and until assuming office was utterly ignorant of the atomic bomb project, but he was to prove that sometimes even the most inexperienced of people can rise to the occasion and serve their cause or country well.

American and British troops were soon storming over western Germany. Thousands of civilians were also now fleeing westwards towards them, in order to be under their rule and not that of the dreaded Soviets. Similarly, although Hitler on 19 March ordered a policy of destruction and of fighting to the end, many Germans, especially those fighting Western forces, did not obey his decree. The endgame was slowly coming into sight, with some 300,000 Germans being captured by Patton's Third Army alone. Against the Red Army, however, the Germans fought fanatically.

The Allies were now also discovering the concentration camps. On 4 April, Americans came across a camp on the edge of Buchenwald and on 15 April British forces arrived at Belsen. While those in the West did not match the full horror of the extermination camps in Poland being uncovered by the Red Army, they were certainly awful. The thousands of victims now met by Western forces were skeletal creatures, barely alive. Tragically, many died soon after being freed, with fourteen thousand dying at Belsen alone despite all the efforts of their British liberators to help them.

The Allies had not fought the war for the Jews, but when the death camps were found, the revulsion was total and understandable. Some Allied troops shot the SS guards out of hand, and a new moral sense of how terrible the Nazis had been now pervaded the Allies as the war came to a close. The concentration camps were rightly to loom large at the war crimes trials at Nuremburg.

On 25 April, Soviet and American troops met at Torgau on the Elbe. The officers of the various units met formally – and on camera – the following day. It was a tense moment as no one was sure how to behave, and of course the Red Army troops probably feared retribution for meeting up with their co-belligerent, but capitalist, American allies. Nonetheless, it was a deeply symbolic moment, proof of temporary unity among the troops of two very different countries united for four years in pursuit of a common foe.

This had taken the USA well into the territory assigned at Yalta to the Soviets. Churchill hoped that the West could keep what the Americans had captured. But by this time, with victory in Europe so close and with the need, as then thought by the USA, to send thousands of troops to conquer Japan, the president and his advisers decided that the agreed zone borders should be maintained. While Churchill, in a potential plan to go to war with the Soviets, codenamed *Unthinkable*, was prepared to contemplate war with the USSR, he was very much on his own. But the decision to wait and let the Soviets seize Prague when Patton could easily have liberated the Czech capital was surely a shame, and one that was much rued in the forty-one years (1948–89) that the Czechs spent under Soviet rule.

By the end of April, the end really was in sight. On 29 April, Hitler finally decided to do the right thing by his mistress and married Eva Braun. His last testament was a rant of hostility against his lifelong foes, especially to Jews. Then the next day he and Eva Hitler committed suicide in their bunker. The Fuehrer was dead. (Years later bits of his skull were found, proof that he really was dead and not in some Latin American hideaway.)

The same day, Mussolini and his mistress Clara Petacci, both of whom had been captured by partisans on 28 April, were shot and their bodies hung upside down in Milan. Now Stalin was the only dictator left alive, and his moment of glory was about to come.

The capture of Berlin and V-E Day

In Europe, the Allies stuck firmly to unconditional surrender; attempts, for example, by Himmler to surrender only to the Western Allies proved abortive. In Italy, the Germans attempted to negotiate surrender through Allen Dulles of the OSS (the precursor to the CIA, which Dulles later directed). But the Soviets got to hear of it and Molotov was furious. In the end, German forces surrendered unconditionally to the USA and British on 29 April, with hostilities formally ceasing three days later. But in effect, for nearly one million Wehrmacht and other forces, the war was over.

The flowery historian Alan Clark referred to Hitler's senior henchmen as the *diadochi*, the ancient Greek name bestowed upon the principal lieutenants of Alexander the Great. Several of them would have loved to succeed Hitler as Fuehrer, though that title was for all intents and purposes now utterly meaningless. But despite the longings of Goering and of Himmler, none of them was deemed worthy and Hitler nominated Grand Admiral Doenitz, the commander of the U-boats, who now inherited the poisoned chalice.

On 2 May, General Vasily Chuikov accepted the German surrender in Berlin. A symbolic photo was taken of the victorious Red Army troops placing the Red Flag on the shattered ruins of the former Reichstag.

Then on 2 May, German troops in the Netherlands, Denmark and northern Germany surrendered. Norway would be occupied until the end of the war. An attempt by the German military to surrender only to the West again proved futile, so that when Field Marshal Jodl went to Eisenhower's temporary headquarters in Rheims, it was to sign unconditional surrender, which he did on 7 May. However, the USSR insisted on its own capitulation, and this took place with Zhukov in command of the Red Army in the ruins of Berlin on 8 May.

With the surrender now having happened in both places, V-E Day – Victory in Europe – could finally be celebrated on 8 May. In London, thousands of people cheered outside Buckingham Palace, the roar becoming substantially louder when Churchill appeared triumphant on the balcony. The war in Europe was over. But the war against Japan was still raging. Allied forces in Asia lamented as their comrades continued to die in battle.

8

The War in Asia and the Pacific 1943–1945

The war in China: Ichigo and its consequences

This book emphasises the conflict that took place outside Europe, and outsideWestern Europe in particular. But even books that mention the war in Asia and the Pacific and the conflict about Japan often omit any reference to the titanic struggle that took place in China. For example, in one of the better popular books, the author, on getting to 1944 says, 'I haven't said a lot about China to this point.' He then proceeds to do so in relation to US policy: the massive Japanese offensive of that year, *Ichigo*, is never mentioned by name.

In 1941, Roosevelt was lauding Generalissimo Chiang as a worthy war leader, the hero of a future great power. By 1944, however, American public opinion had come to see that the much-vaunted Kuomintang army, while indeed vast on paper was, to use an expression invented in another Chinese context, no more than a paper tiger. Chiang and Mao were still more interested in the civil war that would take place after victory, and neither of them was truly interested in fighting the common Japanese enemy if it would weaken their own side in what they regarded as the truly important conflict that could then follow.

Nor did the Americans sent to China agree with each other. General Chennault, the commander of the American Flying Tigers squadrons, was still convinced that air power could win the struggle against the Japanese. His army equivalent, General 'Vinegar Joe' Stillwell, in theoretical charge of Chinese troops as well as of US personnel in that country, seemed to be fighting as fierce a metaphorical war against his own side as he was a real battle against the Japanese. The situation in all senses was far from promising.

Then in April 1944, the Japanese launched *Ichigo* against the Nationalist forces, their largest military operation yet to take place in China. Over 510,000 troops took part (five-sixths of the entire Japanese occupation force of China). The Chinese were swiftly routed and worse still from the American point of view, the air bases that the USAAF had hoped to use against Japan were also destroyed. Some 300,000 of Chiang's forces were wiped out, and any chance of China being a major player in the war ended then as well.

Historians differ on how much difference the war in China made compared to that in the Pacific. The scale of *Ichigo* and the fact that it denied an American base in China physically close to the Japanese home islands, show that it did make an enormous impact, not just in tying down hundreds of thousands of Japanese troops but also in determining that it was from the American effort in the Pacific that the main assault against Japan would have to come.

The battle for Saipan and a terrible way of war

By April 1944, the US cross-Pacific attack had already reached the key Marshall Islands. On 15 June, the first wave of invasion took place on the island of Saipan, in the Marianas. This attack, three weeks long, shows the sheer brutality of the war in the Pacific that, while not matching the total carnage of the Eastern Front, certainly came close. Some thirty thousand Japanese troops died, many thousands in suicide attacks against the Americans. There were fourteen thousand US casualties. But what made Saipan truly barbaric was that seven thousand Japanese civilians died by throwing themselves off the edge of cliffs, despite being begged not to by the horrified Americans. The nearby naval battle of the Philippine Sea went down in US folklore as the 'Great Marianas Turkey Shoot', so easy did it become for the Americans to down not just Japanese battleships but hundreds of enemy planes as well.

SUICIDE AT MARPI POINT

The suicide at Marpi Point on Saipan of so many thousands of Japanese civilians horrified the Americans who witnessed it, including the influential *Time* magazine journalist Robert Sherrod, whose article *The Nature of the Enemy* transformed US thinking on the Japanese against whom they were fighting.

The civilians who killed themselves either hurled themselves off the 200-foot cliff or used grenades to blow themselves (and their children) to smithereens. Japanese soldiers actively encouraged the suicides and attempted to kill civilians who wished to surrender.

The Japanese had been indoctrinated that all Americans were barbarians, who would rape the women and kill and torture the men. This seemed ingrained in the national psyche from years of propaganda, and the Americans realised that this was the case, however much they did to preserve civilian life and to treat their captives according to the rules of war. (American journalists and soldiers witnessed scenes of Japanese soldiers beheading similar prisoners en masse, including on Saipan.)

One result was an absolute determination in the US High Command to get on with and to finish the war. There was natural grave concern about mass suicides on the Japanese main islands – indeed, they discovered Japanese propaganda lauding the Saipan suicides as honourable role models. In turn, this helped to create the mentality that led to Hiroshima – anything to end the war against a people so incomprehensible and seemingly barbaric as soon as possible was a risk worth taking.

It also, as Michael Burleigh has shown, much increased a sense of reciprocal racism on the part of the US Marines, who would tell journalists that it was easy to kill Japanese soldiers because they hated them so much.

Interestingly, this feeling of the enemy as some barbaric 'other' out there was not felt by the Americans fighting against the Germans, who were racially the same. (When it came to their Western enemies the Germans kept to the Geneva Convention.) Not until the discovery of the death camps and of the Nazi mass extermination of the Jews did feelings of revulsion match those felt by the US Marines in the Pacific.

In July 1944, Roosevelt flew to Pearl Harbor to meet with his two key commanders. The US Navy (including Admirals King and Nimitz) wanted to bypass the Philippines and go straight for a course that would lead directly to the conquest of Japan, via Taiwan. MacArthur was conscious of his pledge to return to the Philippines and wanted to capture them first.

Militarily, King's plan made much more strategic sense, and might well have shortened the war. However, with the November 1944 presidential election looming, Roosevelt felt it more prudent politically to go with MacArthur, the hero of 1941, and take the longer route via the Philippines. How much longer this made the war is a moot point, since none of the protagonists in 1944 knew that the war with Japan would end with the atomic bombs (and with Roosevelt having died before victory). Whether or not MacArthur – who hated the president – and Roosevelt also made some kind of political deal, is not known. Either way, the course of the war in the Pacific was now set.

'Bloody Nose Ridge', Peleliu

The American invasion of the Palau islands now proceeded, and the fight for Peleliu, which possessed an important airstrip, is indicative of how the war would continue to unfold. The tiny island took over a month to subdue, with 6,526 Marine casualties (including 1,252 deaths) and another 3,278 losses from the 81st Division, which had been brought in to help finish the job.

Just to give an idea of the scale of the fighting in the Pacific war, the number of US servicemen killed or injured in taking the tiny island of Peleliu, and its main beach, (nicknamed 'Bloody Nose Ridge' by the Marines) was 9,615 casualties. This was in excess of all the American, Canadian and British casualties combined on D-Day. Not surprisingly, US historian Donald Miller has described it as 'the most savage battle of the Pacific' theatre. Over one third of the US Marine Corps division attacking the island were wiped out, and Japanese resistance on Bloody Nose Ridge killed sixty percent of the American invasion force. The island itself is only five square miles in size, and if one considers that fewer Allied troops died to capture all the Normandy beaches, Omaha included, over a far wider land area, the sheer ferocity and death toll of the island can be grasped. The Marines who survived put up a sign: 'We will build a barrier across the Pacific with our bodies'. On Peleliu they did just that.

It was a tremendously high death toll, and this attrition rate, although one that could just be afforded by the USA, was on the scale that made planners think very long and hard on what on earth it would be like to attack the Japanese home islands themselves. From such statistics can be seen the road to Hiroshima and an altogether more drastic way of dealing with an enemy that always fought to the death, refusing ever to surrender. Remember, too, when the British and American allies met up in Quebec in September 1944, the clear expectation was that the effective war to finish off Japan would take eighteen months after D-Day. Also, no one at that time knew that the Germans would still be fighting at Christmas.

Leyte and the battle for the Philippines begins

On 20 October 1944, MacArthur finally waded ashore on the Philippine island of Leyte, with much proclamation and fawning press coverage of his successful return. Since the majority of Japanese ground forces were expecting a landing on the main island of Luzon, comparatively few troops were there to oppose him.

But the US Navy nearly threw away the vital naval advantage that it possessed, and with it the vitally needed protection for the invasion forces. The Battle of Leyte Gulf, while well known in the USA, is hardly familiar to British and Europeans, yet it has rightly been called 'the greatest naval battle in history'.

The Japanese fleet had as part of its force the two biggest battleships ever built, the *Yamato* and *Musashi*. Yet this could not prevent the devastating American assault, with no fewer than 225 major ships altogether. Admiral Kinkaid did his duty and irreplaceable Japanese ships were sunk.

But now Admiral Halsey decided to go on an escapade of his own, made worse by internal miscommunication within the US fleet. By the time he had returned to where he should have been if he had obeyed Nimitz's orders correctly, some of the Japanese fleet had been able to escape. (This was therefore nicknamed the 'Battle of Bull's Run' after Halsey's nickname 'Bull'.) But the Battle of Leyte Gulf was unquestionably a great US victory.

By the time that the Americans had finally conquered the island of Leyte, they discovered, too late, that it was unsuitable for airstrips. The conquest of Luzon, with over 250,000 Japanese troops, now became more complicated, and not until the spring of 1945 would most of the main island be liberated. But by then a lot more US soldiers would have died.

Iwo Jima: an iconic battle in the Pacific

The Battle of Iwo Jima has become one of the most iconic of the whole war, largely because of a press photograph taken on Mount Suribachi on 23 February 1945. It shows five US Marines and a medical orderly planting the US flag as if in victory. But it was only on the fourth day of the attack on the island, and only half those in the picture survived to tell the tale. Some 22,000 Japanese troops were still in place, in eighteen miles of bunkers and secure emplacements, ready to fight another day. The photo deserves its fame, but as an account of the actual battle itself it is highly misleading.

The invasion of Iwo Jima, the first part of actual Japanese territory to come under American attack, started on 16 February when the bombardment began, the landings happened on 19 February and the battle continued until 26 or 27 March (depending on when the Japanese stopped fighting). Some 6,821 US Marine Corps soldiers were killed and 363 naval troops – 800 Marines died in the capture of Mount Suribachi alone and 19,217 were seriously injured.

Far worse was the fact that, as on other islands, the Japanese steadfastly refused to surrender, whatever the overwhelming odds. (Lt General Kuribayashi knew the USA as a military attaché there in the late 1920s so understood his attackers.) By the time that the Marines had finally captured the island, well over 21,000 Japanese defenders had died, many taking their own lives rather than agreeing to become prisoners.

The US Army was deeply critical of what they regarded as the cavalier approach to Marine Corps lives taken by the US

Navy – though the sacrifice on Iwo Jima pales into insignificance when compared to the far greater carnage suffered by the Red Army from 1941 onwards. Nevertheless, some units were to lose all their officers or two-thirds and more of their men. But as Max Hastings argues, the capture was inevitable, even if the island was never used as the strategic base for the air offensive against Japan as originally intended. Sometimes war develops an internal logic of its own, and Iwo Jima was to be part of that price.

Now is a good time to mention the little-known book *D-Days in the Pacific* by Donald Miller. There he shows that the kind of amphibious assault we associate with D-Day in Normandy took place well over a hundred times in the Pacific war. The USA had to accomplish a similar feat every time they invaded an island, however great, like Okinawa, or small, such as Iwo Jima or Saipan. (And hence, too, the vital importance of the Seabees or US Naval construction crews as mentioned in the box on unsung heroes of the war in Chapter 6.) Obviously, no single Pacific landing came anywhere close to the scale of Normandy, but cumulatively they were not far off such magnitude. And the Americans were not the only forces fighting the Japanese. So too were many British, Indian, Australian and New Zealand troops.

Burma: the forgotten war

The Americans who fought in the Pacific have long been celebrated in their own country. But British forces which fought outside the Mediterranean (including North Africa) or away from northwest Europe are often forgotten. Consequently, the British and Indian troops who fought tenaciously against the Japanese in Burma often felt that they were the forgotten army. Sadly, this was proved to be the case for another reason. Although they were battling directly against the Japanese, they did not have the strategic significance of the much greater struggle happening between Japan and the USA in the Pacific Ocean.

However, General Sir William Slim, who was to end the war in command of the Fourteenth Army in Burma, has made up for some of this sense of abandonment. He is usually now reckoned by most historians to be the best British commander in the war. As Montgomery's star has waned, Slim's has waxed, and while it might be unfair on other British generals to elevate Slim uniquely to the top position, he certainly deserves the praise that his reputation now receives.

Burma was the route into India for the Japanese, and the original capture of what was still then a part of the British Empire proved remarkably swift. Burma had virtually no strategic or economic importance, but as well as the road into India, control of Burma meant control of what was called the 'Burma Road'. This route has been described as 'the last link between China and the outside world'. Much of this was an air route, known as the 'hump', over which vitally needed supplies could go from British-ruled territory in India to the otherwise utterly isolated Kuomintang Chinese under Chiang Kai-shek.

For this reason, Burma was important to the USA as well as to the British. But all the same, Admiral Mountbatten's Southeast Asia Command (SEAC) was sometimes thus nicknamed 'Save England's Asian Colonies'.

Most of Burma was under Japanese control by May 1942. But even the Japanese found it impossible to get any further. The fact that the British were still able to rule the whole of India with so few troops was always something of complete astonishment to Hitler, who admired Britain for it. But hold it they did, despite the fact that many troops had to be used during the war not so much to fight the Japanese enemy, without, but to crush the Indians, who naturally wanted independence, within. Neither Roosevelt nor Chiang Kai-shek appreciated Churchill's stubborn obstinacy on this issue. Nor, it should also be added, did Churchill's wartime coalition colleagues in the Labour Party (most notably Sir Stafford Cripps, the maverick politician whose mission to solve the Indian independence issue was arguably sabotaged by Churchill himself).

India paid a huge price for its loyalty to the Raj. Some three million Indian soldiers fought alongside the British, not just in South Asia but also in Europe (as those who have seen *The English Patient* will recall). Most of these had British commanders, of whom Field Marshal Auchinleck was to command troops in the Middle East and Slim, who led his forces to victory in 1945.

Some of the strangest soldiers fought in Burma, including the Chindits. These were British-commanded jungle warriors led by the profoundly eccentric (and perhaps insane) General Orde Wingate. The Chindits, a precursor to today's Special Forces, were immensely audacious, surviving in conditions that would have killed most other soldiers, and yet managed to do the enemy real damage. (The actual origin of the SAS was in the North Africa campaigns, with soldiers of similar unconventional outlook and great skill.)

The troops in Burma always felt unloved. Because of the enormous difficulty in supplying them, and the uniquely arduous conditions in which they fought, this is alas not surprising.

But what is significant is that while British attempts (using mainly Indian troops and also those special semi-mercenary units, the Gurkhas from Nepal) to seize back control of Burma usually failed, so too did Japanese efforts to penetrate through the jungle from the other side and into the Raj itself. Theoretically, American troops under China-based commanders such as Generals Stillwell and Chennault were also involved in the struggle in Burma, but in their case the main priority was always the gigantic battle between the Japanese and those Chinese forces under Chiang Kai-shek.

As Evan Mawdsley puts it, 'Burma was a place where Tokyo's grand strategy worked; the Japanese Army established a defensive perimeter, and the Allies lacked the co-ordinated will and the means to breach it.'

Not until well into 1944 were Slim's forces finally able to dislodge the Japanese. And this, Evan Mawdsley has correctly argued, was possible because of the folly of the Japanese in March 1944, when they decided to launch a major attack on the Raj, which then proceeded utterly to fail.

Some accounts of the fighting are straight out of Somerset Maugham. In one garrison town, the British troops gallantly held out in a tennis court against waves of Japanese attacks until help finally arrived. The sieges of the two key cities of Imphal and Kohima proved to be a total fiasco as the British/Indian forces refused to budge and managed to succeed in repelling the enemy assault.

In turn, Slim's forces were able to counter-attack in July 1944, and in essence they never had to retreat. While American historians might argue that the Japanese losses at Leyte Gulf were greater, and Australians would argue that the defeat of the invaders in New Guinea was much more important, one British historian has suggested that the loss of Burma was 'probably the Japanese Army's worst defeat in a land battle during World War II'. Jungle conditions continued to prove unbelievably harsh, but by May 1945, the Burmese capital Rangoon was back in Allied hands. All the intense British and Indian loss and suffering had, in the end, proved worth it after all.

Meanwhile back in the Pacific

While marines were dying to capture Iwo Jima, others were fighting to recapture the Philippines. Max Hastings has suggested that much of this was not militarily necessary for the defeat of Japan, but was tied up with the egotism of General MacArthur and his wish for revenge. The decision of the Japanese to commit to kamikaze tactics made this much more hazardous for the Americans. In Manila, Japanese forces carried out wholesale slaughter of innocent Filipino citizens. While most of the main island of Luzon was in US hands by March, some of the Japanese held out until August 1945 and the surrender of their country.

The recapture of the Philippines was certainly important – and the USA, so unlike the French in Indochina, decided to give independence to the colony the next year (with the new president being someone who had collaborated with the Japanese). But is MacArthur, like similar self-publicist Montgomery, an overrated commander? It is hard to tell.

Getting closer to Japan

Meanwhile, the real struggle for the defeat of Japan was continuing, under the indisputably able command of Admiral Nimitz. The next necessary target was Okinawa, an island of 450 square miles, in the Ryuku Archipelago and well within bomber reach of the Japanese main islands. The capture of Okinawa was critical because by now the Americans were bombing much of the Japanese mainland, including some devastating raids on the capital itself, Tokyo.

HAMBURG AND TOKYO

The bombing of Hamburg in 1943 – rather aptly named *Operation Gomorrah* – resulted in the death of over 42,000 people. (By contrast, the more infamous raid on Dresden in 1945 had fewer deaths.) Today, the bombing by the Allies of German civilians in World War II is regarded very differently from how it appeared at the time, and is now, rightly many would argue, looked upon as barbaric and unnecessary.

However, the raids on Japan killed far more people and yet have been less controversial in historical debate. Well over 100,000 were killed in the innocently named *Operation Meetinghouse* firebomb raid in early 1945. Since the death toll at Hiroshima was spread over time (with people surviving the blast itself and dying later of radiation poisoning) one can say that the fire raid on Tokyo killed more people in one day than were killed by the initial explosion at Hiroshima. (And some 40,000 more died in Tokyo than at Nagasaki.)

So first, the firebombing of Tokyo was far worse than that of either Hamburg or Dresden. Second, it was almost as bad as the atomic bomb on Hiroshima, since many of the survivors were rendered homeless and huge swathes of the city were destroyed.

Why therefore is Tokyo not as infamous as the raids on Germany or the two atomic bombs later in 1945? Historians are now pondering this very issue, but many decades after the event. Surely a Japanese life is as worthwhile or important as a German? A civilian in Tokyo does not differ from one in Hamburg. And if Bishop Bell of Chichester was right about bombing non-military targets over Germany, then would not the same apply to Japan? If we are to take the war in Asia as seriously as we should then these are questions that need to be asked.

Unlike Iwo Jima, which was arguably not bombarded enough before the American forces landed, Okinawa was subject to full naval attack first. But even then it took the invasion force some two whole months to subdue the main 120,000 Japanese forces heavily ensconced in their defensive positions and a further month to get them out altogether – from 1 April to 21 June. Worse still, kamikaze attacks knocked out or disabled some 245 American ships although it was a conventional air attack that caused major fire damage to the carrier *Franklin* with the loss of 725 lives. Not since Pearl Harbor had the US Navy lost so much or so many – some 5,000 were killed. Over 75,000 American casualties had resulted by the time the island was finally overcome, with nearly 8,000 army or marine deaths. All this is not to forget the 42,000 to 150,000 civilian deaths (and for that

LIES AND STATISTICS

The old saying 'there are lies, damned lies and statistics' is very true of wartime statistics. In writing about Okinawa, one reliable source says that some 75,000 US forces suffered casualties, but another quotes a figure of 65,000 – a difference of 10,000 people. And a source used by Yale academic Paul Kennedy has the refreshing honesty to say that between 42,000 and 150,000 Okinawa civilians were killed in the two horrific months of fighting. These two last figures are widely divergent, and the main source books this work has used are wise: one does not provide any figures at all and the other says that the lower death toll is much too high. Most seem to agree that at least ninety percent of the 120,000 Japanese defenders died, many by committing suicide.

We know that 7,613 American service personnel died, which is a very high figure for such an island.

Can we ever get precise figures? On the Eastern Front between Germany and the USSR, for instance, even best guess figures have been decades in coming, as more archives are opened to tell us more of the truth than we were allowed to know by the evasive and secretive Soviets at the time.

This book has used many sources, so the statistics given here might not be those in other works. In the end, we will probably never know the exact details of deaths and injuries in many of the famous battles of the conflict. But what we do know is that totals run into millions and that World War II saw more carnage than any other conflict in world history, whatever the precise numbers might be.

discrepancy see the box on statistics) – whichever figure is near the truth it was a hideous death toll.

Finally, as Anthony Beevor so rightly says:

> The capture of Okinawa may not have hastened the end of the war. Its prime aim was to serve as a base for the invasion of Japan, but the suicidal nature of its defence certainly concentrated minds in Washington on the next steps to consider.

If anything that last sentence is an understatement. It now brings us to the deeply controversial end of the war against Japan. For if the capture of an island cost that much – including civilian deaths – what on earth would the invasion of the main islands cost in terms of Allied military fatalities and Japanese civilian lives?

The Japanese endgame: the great debate

The decision to drop atomic bombs upon the two Japanese cities of Hiroshima and Nagasaki was probably the most controversial of the war. It has allowed Japanese to get away with arguing that the Nanjing massacre and other atrocities committed by their forces in Asia are somehow balanced by what the Allies inflicted upon their country in 1945.

The case for dropping the bombs is a complex one and is hard to compress. Those interested in pursuing this further could read the final chapters in Max Hasting's book *Nemesis*, which shows that rather than a sudden decision being made, the path to Hiroshima and Nagasaki was elongated over several months, particularly from June 1945 onwards. He also emphasises Truman's complete inexperience. The president had only just come to office, following Roosevelt's death, and his predecessor had excluded him from all knowledge of the Manhattan Project, the codename for the atomic bomb project. The final decision was therefore taken by a complete political neophyte who, as Hastings shows, chose in his subsequent memoirs to obfuscate the reasons that prevailed back in the summer of 1945 for the fatal act.

Hastings also makes two points seldom made, both of which are very important.

First, the Soviet invasion of Manchuria, if it had continued for longer, would certainly have killed far more Japanese than those who died in the atomic blasts. Most historians ignore or belittle the powerful Red Army offensive against Japan fought on Chinese/Manchurian soil, and the wholesale rape and pillaging carried out against wholly innocent Chinese civilians. Hastings does not make this mistake and nor should we.

Second – and not all will agree here – he argues that had the war continued, considerably more Japanese citizens would have starved to death from the Allied blockade or been incinerated in what would have been a continuation of the American firebombing of Japanese cities. Indeed, it is possible that far more civilians would have died by this means than from atomic fallout.

Hastings does not go along with the usual rationale – from Truman to historians ever since – that argues that more American soldiers would have died in the invasion (*Operation Olympic*) and civilians caught in the inevitable crossfire of war. His thesis is that firebombing and starvation, along with the massive Japanese military losses against the Americans and British, would eventually have ended the war anyway, but much later and with far greater loss of life.

The argument that America might not have needed to launch a ground invasion may or may not be justifiable. But Marshall was still counting on launching *Olympic*. The argument that the Soviet war against Japan in China and the rapid starvation of countless Japanese combine to a far worse death toll than Hiroshima and Nagasaki does have considerable leverage as a case for using the bombs.

And there is one final merit – the 'Sir Harry Hinsley thesis', named after a British wartime intelligence officer and subsequent historian at Cambridge. So terrible were the effects of the bombs and so evident was the destruction that ever to use them again as rational weapons in war became completely unthinkable, however terrible the Cold War became. World War III and nuclear Armageddon never took place. If it had, of course, the death toll in Japan would have been minuscule in comparison and all humanity might have been destroyed

Much depends on whether or not the Japanese would have surrendered without the bombs having to be used. Here we get into a historical and interpretative minefield. This is a battle among historians that has lasted almost ever since the decision in August 1945 to drop the two bombs, and especially since it became known that the USA was able to decrypt the Japanese diplomatic ciphers at that time. That means in effect that the US government, now under the new president Harry S. Truman was able to read all the Japanese government decision-making processes simultaneously with the Japanese leaders themselves.

One of the major problems was that the Japanese peace party, who knew that their country was defeated and that the war should end, had the same utterly unrealistic aims as their equivalents among the July plotters in Germany in 1944. They wanted, for example, Japan to keep both Manchuria and Korea, and for no blame to be attached to Japan for having been effectively at war since 1931. There was no possible way in which the Americans and their allies could ever agree to such demands.

One non-negotiable item for Japan was the position of the emperor. This divided the Americans (and British, who were less important in such discussions) since for some of the American decision makers Emperor Hirohito was the only person who could deliver surrender, while for others he was a war criminal and to do a deal through him would be to abandon the whole concept of unconditional surrender.

JAPAN AND UNCONDITIONAL SURRENDER

At Casablanca, Roosevelt had made it very clear that the Allies would accept only unconditional surrender – there was to be no repetition of Germany in 1918.

As we saw above, this created problems when Italy wished to change sides in 1943, following the overthrow of Mussolini. One could argue that the delays caused by the Allied doctrine gave the Germans enough time to send forces to Italy big enough to prevent the Allies from seizing the country.

In the case of Japan, there can be no doubt that the surrender was actually entirely conditional, and was made on the explicit understanding that the emperor would be retained after Japanese capitulation. When many leading war criminals were put on trial by the victorious Americans, all of them decided on principle to do everything to exonerate the emperor and keep his wartime activities firmly out of their evidence. Hirohito died peacefully in his bed in 1989.

Since he ended the war by his declaration, it could be said that his action saved millions of lives – those of his fellow countrymen and women who would have been killed during the invasion or committed mass suicide (as thousands did in Saipan) and those of the American forces who would have been obliged to fight every inch to capture the main islands in a way that could have made their capture of some of the smaller Pacific islands look mild in comparison.

Nonetheless, in twenty-first-century Japan, while the emperor is in effect a cipher, leading politicians still revere many a category A war criminal buried in shrines as national heroes. Japan has not been forced to undergo anything like the repentance and self-reflection of Germany. While hundreds of thousands of Japanese died in Allied bombing raids, the main islands were not physically conquered in the way that the Third Reich was comprehensively invaded and flattened. Now that Japan is becoming nationalistic and assertive again, but without the kind of memory and inward change of post-1945 Germany, the conditional nature of Japan's surrender still haunts us.

This debate went on in Washington for some time, and what we should remember is that a similar debate regarding what on earth to do next was happening in Tokyo. The emperor was slowly coming around to the side of the peace party. However, the war faction viewed any kind of surrender as unthinkable and the very basest treachery. They were adamant in wanting to fight on to the very last.

It was the knowledge of the existence of such people that had much influence in Washington when the military planners realised how many hundreds of thousands of US forces would die if *Operation Olympic*, the invasion of the first of the two Japanese main islands (Kyushu and Shikoku), and then *Operation Coronet* (the invasion of Honshu) was to take place. They estimated at least 350,000 deaths for the two islands and maybe up to a million or more British and American military deaths overall.

Furthermore, as Anthony Beevor reminds us, the very high civilian death toll in Okinawa also led the US leadership to ponder how many innocent civilians would die in the invasion process.

Not only that, but as historians now point out, the Allies had discovered two truly horrific things: first that the Japanese were close to producing biological weapons (the infamous Unit 731) but also that their troops had, in all parts of the Pacific, been active cannibals, and that many Allied prisoners had not only been killed but also eaten by their captors. As one historian rightly puts it, not even the SS committed such atrocities. Not surprisingly, the Allies were disgusted by the sheer scale of the barbarity of their opponents.

CANNIBALS AND KAMIKAZES

It has been suggested that as many as sixty percent of the Japanese forces who died in World War II did so as a result of starvation. Countless island garrisons were cut off from any food supplies by very effective American submarine warfare, and therefore the troops stationed in such places had grossly inadequate nutrition.

Japanese forces were notorious for their cannibalism, with different nicknames for their human food source depending upon the victim's ethnic origin. The discovery of this behaviour disgusted the Americans fighting against them beyond measure. This, along with the total refusal of Japanese soldiers ever to surrender even against the most overwhelming odds and certain defeat meant that US forces increasingly found it hard to treat their Japanese enemies as fully human, as Michael Burleigh shows clearly in his book *Moral Combat*.

All this, plus the regular use of kamikaze (= divine wind) suicide pilots against American ships had a powerful influence on US thinking towards Japan. As Anthony Beevor argues, such extraordinary tactics – quite unthinkable to Western minds – led inexorably towards thinking of a drastic way of ending the war, especially since no effective shield against kamikaze attacks was ever discovered. The road to the atomic bomb became clearer every day that the fight against Japan continued.

The Soviets enter the Pacific war

At both the Yalta Conference and again at Potsdam in July 1945, Stalin had made clear that he would keep his promise to attack Japan as soon as the war in Europe was over. He now fulfilled that oath. On 9 August, over 1.6 million Red Army troops invaded Japanese-held territory in China/Manchuria over a 5,000-mile wide front. Since many of the Japanese Kwantung Army troops were underequipped and not used to fighting first-rate enemies, they were slaughtered or captured in the hundreds of thousands. Very soon, Soviet forces had traversed hundreds of miles and taken huge swathes of territory. The Red Army was quickly occupying northern Korea as well and, but for American protest, would soon have been occupying actual Japanese territory. Soviet troops soon carried out the same widespread rape and pillage on innocent civilians that they committed in the West.

Most of the Japanese peace feelers had been through the USSR, with the former in ignorance of Soviet plans to end the neutrality pact and join the USA and Britain in the war in East Asia. This avenue of trying to get a negotiated deal, on the basis that the Soviets would be kinder, was now firmly closed. It also terrified many of the Japanese who had hitherto thought that their country could continue the war.

The two atomic bombs were dropped upon Japan on 6 August (on Hiroshima, with over 100,000 immediate deaths) and on 9 August (on Nagasaki, with over 35,000 people killed outright). Prior to that, on 26 July, the victorious Allies issued the Potsdam Declaration demanding, in effect, Japanese surrender. The different factions within Tokyo had effectively ignored this demand. This was especially true of the hardliners who, as Ewan Mawdsley has pointed out, had a case that the Japanese defences were strong enough to hold out for a long while if necessary.

Forests of paper have been consumed on what it was that finally persuaded the Japanese to surrender. For some, it was unquestionably the Soviet entry into the war and the immediate success of Red Army troops against Japanese forces. For others, the complete horror of the American weapons was the key factor – though we must not forget that the firebombing of Tokyo did not have that many fewer civilian deaths than the single blast at Hiroshima.

The Japanese Government was for a while deadlocked. But in the end the will of the emperor prevailed. This was a close run thing, as extremist hardliners tried to launch a coup against Hirohito. He had to hide, with his court chamberlain, in order to avoid the plotters, who committed suicide when their plan failed. On 15 August, the emperor, using the very formal and stilted language of court Japanese, ordered his country and its forces to surrender. His wonderful euphemism that things had developed not necessarily to Japan's advantage may have sounded strange but it did the trick. The war was over.

Formal surrender did not come until 2 September in Tokyo, on board the *USS Missouri* (a ship named after the new American president's home state). The conditional nature of Japan's surrender has proved controversial, since the country was able to keep

Hirohito as its head of state – albeit after he renounced his divine status – despite his deeds during the war.

The most bloodthirsty war in history was now fully over. Germany and Japan were both occupied and defeated countries. But as the history of the Cold War years shows, for millions around the world, the peace would be a bittersweet experience.

Conclusion

Who Won the War?

Who won World War II?

This is the classic university essay question. On the face of it, the winners were the USSR and the USA. These massive countries emerged as the two superpowers as a result of the war. They became the principal protagonists of the Cold War that followed and which lasted all the way down to 1989/91.

That is the obvious answer, but is it too easy?

For a while after 1991, the USA was called the hyperpower and the era of 1991–2001 was called the unipolar moment, once the bipolar US–Soviet age of 1945–91 was over. Now with the rise of the BRIC countries (Brazil, Russia, India, China – especially the last) we are living in a multipolar time in which several nations could emerge as superpowers by the middle to end of the twenty-first century.

But as Evan Mawdsley reminds us, both the USA and the USSR have proved the point made by Yale historian Paul Kennedy as far back as 1987 that all major hegemonic powers sooner or later burn themselves out, from the empire of Spain down to the British Empire. (And one can now add that while Russia is a BRIC, the old USSR evaporated just four years after Kennedy's prognosis.) This is because of what he calls imperial overstretch, of great powers ruining themselves after ceasing to be able to maintain their international dominant status.

America became the world's policeman in 1945. Britain was bankrupt and began to abandon its empire from 1947. France was defeated in Vietnam and then Algeria, and in 1991 the

Soviet Union was dissolved, after their failure to control not just Afghanistan but their de facto empire in Central Europe.

But now, in the twenty-first century, even American predominance looks very overstretched.

Japan and Germany, however, with no post-1945 imperial possibilities opened to them, have done well, Japanese stagnation in more recent years notwithstanding. They have no expensive overseas military costs to bear, since their constitutions understandably ban the use of international armed force. While predictions of Japanese superpower status in the 1980s have proved exaggerated, neither Japan nor Germany is facing the very real loss of power that now confronts the USA. Germany has become a leader in the European Union and both Japan and Germany are members of the G8 club of richest nations.

(This is hopefully a bipartisan analysis, and as commentators such as Fareed Zakaria remind us, the absolute decline of the USA could be a very long way off yet.) Russia now has borders in Europe narrower than it has had since the eighteenth century – since 1721. Long term it is heavily dependent on the price of its natural resources. China, the country that suffered so appallingly during the war, may become the superpower of the second half of the twenty-first century. In which case, the world in which future generations will inhabit will be a very different one from the Western-dominated world of the twentieth century.

And as for the future international status of the USA, only time will tell. But from 1945 it was the indispensable power, and in 1941–5 it rescued the world.

Selective Chronology

It would be possible to have an entry for every day from 1937 to1945. However, that would be longer than this book, so what follows is a key events chronology of some of the more important dates.

1937

July: Marco Polo Bridge incident and the beginning of the war
December: The Nanking Massacre

1938

March: Germany takes over Austria peacefully
September – October: The Munich Crisis

1939

March: The Germans invade the rump of Czechoslovakia
20–31 August: Zhukov beats the Japanese at Khalkhin Gol
23 August: The Nazi–Soviet Pact
1 September: The invasion of Poland
3 September: France and Britain declare war on Germany
17 September: The Soviets invade their side of Poland
November: The Winter War (the Soviet invasion of Finland)

1940

March 1940: End of the Winter War

April: German invasion of Denmark and Norway

10 May: German invasion of France and the Benelux countries

10 May: Winston Churchill becomes prime minister of Britain

26 May: Evacuation of the British Expeditionary Force from Dunkirk

21 June: France signs an armistice with Germany

10 July: Start of the Battle of Britain

23 July: Soviets annex the three Baltic States

12 August: Britain and USA sign the Atlantic Charter

7 September: Beginning of the London Blitz

27 September: Tripartite Axis Pact (Germany, Italy, Japan)

28 October: The Italians invade Greece

December 1940 to February 1941: *Operation Compass* in North Africa

1941

12 February: Rommel lands in North Africa

11 March: Lend-lease signed into law in the USA

6 April: *Operation Marita* begins: the Nazi invasion of Yugoslavia and Greece

May: Battle for Crete

October 1941 to February 1942: Battle for Moscow

22 June: *Operation Barbarossa*: the Germans invade the USSR

7 December: Pearl Harbor

8 December: Britain and the USA at war with Japan

11 December: Hitler declares war on the USA

1942

20 January: The Wannsee Conference on the Final Solution

26 January: US forces begin to land in the United Kingdom

8–15 February: Siege and capture of Singapore

April: Visit to the UK by George Marshall and Harry Hopkins

12 March: MacArthur leaves the Philippines for Australia

4–8 May: Battle of Coral Sea

12–28 May: Second Battle of Kharkov

4–5 June: Battle of Midway

22 June: Germans capture Tobruk

August 1942 to February 1943: The siege of Stalingrad

August 1942 to February 1943: Guadalcanal campaign

October to November: Second Battle of El Alamein

8 November: US troops land in North Africa

1943

January: The US–UK Casablanca Conference

May: End of the war in North Africa

9 July: US–UK invasion of Sicily

July–August: Battle of Kursk

8 September: Italian surrender

November to December: The Tehran Conference

1944

April to June 1944: Battle of Kohima

6 June: D–Day: Western Allies land in Normandy

15 June to 9 July: Battle of Saipan

22 June to 19 August: Red Army's *Operation Bagration*

20 July: Failed assassination of Hitler

1 August to 2 October: The Warsaw uprising

25 August: Paris liberated

23–26 October: Battle of Leyte Gulf

December: Battle of the Bulge

1945

4–11 February: Stalin, Churchill and Roosevelt at Yalta

13–14 February: Allied air raid on Dresden

23 February: Iwo Jima captured

7 March: Bridge at Remagen taken

9–10 March: Firebombing of Tokyo

1 April to 20 May: Battle for Okinawa

20 April to 2 May: Battle for Berlin

30 April: Suicide of Adolf Hitler

7 May: Unconditional surrender of Germany

8 May: Victory in Europe Day

6 August: First atom bomb on Hiroshima

9 August: Second atom bomb on Nagasaki

15 August: Victory over Japan Day

2 September: Formal Japanese surrender and end of World War II

Further Reading

Some essential reading

There must be thousands of books written about World War II. Thankfully, in recent years some excellent single volume books have appeared, of which a selection appears below. Mawdsley's book gives a significant new perspective on the war that is highly credible, especially on the Asian aspects of war. Beevor's work is most helpful on the latest thinking on the Eastern Front. I have selected more recent books where possible otherwise this list would be impossibly long.

Alanbrooke, Field Marshal Lord, *War Diaries 1939-1945*, London: Weidenfeld and Nicolson, 2001

Bard, Mitchell, *World War II*, 3rd edn New York: Alpha, 2012

Beevor, Anthony, *The Second World War*, London: Phoenix, 2012

Binns and Wood (eds), *The Second World War in Colour*, London: Pavilion Books, 1999

Burleigh, Michael, *Moral Combat*, London: HarperPress, 2010

Collingham, Lizzie, *The Taste of War*, London: Allen Lane, 2011

Corrigan, Gordon, *The Second World War*, London: Atlantic Books, 2010

Farmelo, Graham, *Churchill's Bomb*, London: Faber and Faber, 2013

Gilbert, Martin, *The Atlas of the Second World War*, London: Routledge, 2008

Hastings, Michael, *All Hell Let Loose*, London: HarperPress, 2011

Keegan, John, *The Battle for History*, London: Hutchinson, 1995

Kennedy, David, *The Library of Congress World War II Companion*, New York: Simon & Shuster, 2007

Kennedy, Paul, *Engineers of Victory*, London: Random House, 2013

Mawdsley, Evan, *World War II: A New History*, Cambridge: Cambridge University Press, 2009

Overy, Richard, *Why the Allies Won*, London: W W Norton & Company, 1995

Roberts, Andrew, *The Storm of War*, London: Penguin, 2009

Stone, Norman, *World War II: A Short History*, London: Basic Books, 2013

Weinberg, Gerhard, *A World at Arms*, Cambridge: Cambridge University Press, 1994

New thoughts on the Eastern Front

Some fascinating, if controversial, new thinking has appeared in the past few years that puts the Eastern Front into its proper context. Those by Laurence Rees have also been turned into compelling television documentaries of the same name. Those below are for non-specialists.

Bellamy, Chris, *Total War*, London: Hachette, 2007

Davies, Norman, *Europe at War 1939-1945*, London: Macmillan, 2006

Overy, Richard, *Russia's War*, London: Allen Lane/Penguin, 1997

Rees, Laurence, *War of the Century*, London: BBC Books, 1998

Rees, Laurence, *World War II: Behind Closed Doors*, London: BBC Books, 2008

Roberts, Geoffrey, *Stalin's Wars*, New Haven: Yale University Press, 2006

Snyder, Timothy, *Bloodlands: Europe Between Hitler and Stalin*, London: The Bodley Head, 2010

Two major dictionaries on the war: old but still helpful

Bauer, E (ed.), *The History of World War II*, London: Orbis Publishing, 1979

Keegan, John (ed.), *Encyclopedia of World War II*, London: Hamlyn, 1977

Chapter specific books: with preference for the more recent books if possible

The Origins of War

Brendon, Piers, *The Dark Valley*, London: Jonathan Cape, 2000

Carley, Michael Jabara, *1939: The Alliance That Never Was*, Chicago: Ivan R Dee Publisher, 1999

Overy, Richard, *The Road to War*, London: BBC Books/Macmillan (2nd edn), 2009

Reynolds, David, *From Munich to Pearl Harbor*, Chicago: Ivan R Dee, 2001

Steiner, Zara, *The Triumph of the Dark*, Oxford: Oxford University Press, 2011

Sino-Japanese War 1937–41

Colvin, John, *Nomonhan*, London: Quartet Books, 1999

Ienaga, Saburo, *Japan's Last War 1931-1945*, Oxford: Basil Blackwell, 1979

Mitter, Rana, *China's War With Japan 1937-1945*, London: Allen Lane, 2013

The Hinge of War

Horne, Alistair, *To Lose A Battle: France 1940*, London: Macmillan, 1969

Kershaw, Ian, *Fateful Choices*, London: Penguin Press, 2007

Mawsdley, Evan, *December 1941*, London: Yale University Press, 2011

May, Ernest, *Strange Victory: Hitler's Conquest of France*, London: I B Tauris, 2000

The Eastern Front 1941-1943: I have included some academic (Cambridge University Press) books here since I think that they give details not found elsewhere.

Beevor, Anthony, *Stalingrad*, London: Viking, 1998

Braithwaite, Roderic, *Moscow 1941*, London: Profile Books, 2006

Burleigh, Michael, *Germany Turns Eastwards*, London: Pan (2nd edn), 2002

Gorodetsky, Gabriel, *Grand Delusion: Stalin and the German Invasion of Russia*, New Haven: Yale University Press, 1999

Kershaw, Ian, *Hitler, The Germans and the Final Solution*, London: Yale University Press, 2008

Mosier, John, *Deathride: Hitler vs. Stalin*, New York: Simon & Schuster, 2010

Nagorski, Andrew, *The Greatest Battle: The Fight for Moscow 1941-1942*, London: Aurum Press, 2007

Stahel, David, *Operation Barbarossa and Hitler's Defeat in the East*, Cambridge: Cambridge University Press, 2009

Stahel, David, *Kiev 1941*, Cambridge: Cambridge University Press, 2011

Stahel, David, *Operation Typhoon*, Cambridge: Cambridge University Press, 2013

The Asian and Pacific War 1941–4

Ambrose, Hugh, *The Pacific: Hell Was an Ocean Away*, Edinburgh: Canongate, 2010

Morison, Samuel Eliot, *Two Ocean War*, Boston: Little Brown, 1963

The Americans and British in Africa and Europe 1942–4

Dimbleby, David, *Destiny in the Desert*, London: Profile Books, 2012
Holland, James, *Together We Stand*, London: HarperCollins, 2005
Holland, James, *Dam Busters*, London: Bantam Press, 2012

The Road to Berlin: Eastern Front 1944–5

Beevor, Anthony, *Berlin: The Downfall 1945*, London: Viking, 2002
Davies, Norman, *Rising 1944: The Battle for Warsaw*, London: Macmillan, 2003

The End of the War in Western Europe 1944–5

Beevor, Anthony, *D-Day*, London: Viking, 2009
Bennett, Gillian (ed.), *The End of the War in Europe*, London: HMSO, 1996
Hastings, Max, *Overlord*, London: Michael Joseph, 1984
Hastings, Max, *Armageddon: The Battle for Germany*, London: Macmillan, 2004
Holland, James, *Italy's Sorrow*, London: HarperPress, 2008
Kershaw, Ian, *The End: Hitler's Germany 1944-1945*, London: Allen Lane, 2011

The End of the War Against Japan 1944–5

Hastings, Max, *Nemesis: The Battle for Japan 1944-1945*, London: HarperCollins, 2007

Acknowledgements

In most acknowledgments one reads these days, the author's spouse is thanked at the very end. I believe that that is the wrong place – it should always be at the beginning. So I start with profoundest possible thanks to my wife Dr Paulette Moore Catherwood, who has been my constant inspiration, muse, encourager, best friend and support for nearly a quarter century. Without her love and generosity I would never have been able to write anything like as much as I have been privileged to be able to produce, and my thanks and gratitude towards her is thus deep and lifelong.

Warmest thanks, too, to the commissioning editor at Oneworld, Mike Harpley, without whom this book would not have appeared.

I am a very happy member of several splendid academic institutions, to each one of which I am most grateful for helping in the research, providing vitally needed facilities, and for enabling me to learn as much as I have about so many different aspects of World War II. (As always, any faults in this book are my responsibility and not theirs!)

I am writing this in the Roskill Library of the Churchill Archives Centre of Churchill College Cambridge. In addition, it also has the library of the eminent naval historian Captain Stephen Roskill, and it is thus one of the very best places to study the history of World War II.

So I am, as always, profoundly grateful to all the wonderfully kind, patient and ever friendly archives staff, from the director Allen Packwood on through to all the full-time employees here:

Natalie Adams, Andrew Riley, Sophie Bridges, Katharine Thomson, Sarah Lewery, Julie Sanderson, Emily Morris, Gemma Cook and Liz Yamada.

This will be the fifth book that I have had the pleasure of writing here since my ties with the college began.

I am also profoundly thankful to Major General James Balfour and Julia Weston of the Winston Churchill Memorial Trust for choosing me as a travelling fellow for 2010, giving me the fabulous opportunity to spend time in invaluable archives in the USA.

This book is the second work I have been able to complete with a grant from the Royal Literary Fund. I am most grateful to Hugh Bicheno, the distinguished military historian, for putting me in touch with them and to Eileen Gunn, their administrator, for making it possible for me to have a three-year living grant to write books.

I have the honour of being linked here in Cambridge to two other colleges: St Edmund's, where membership of the SCR is a social delight and to Homerton where I have had the delight of supervising bright undergraduates on British history 1867–2007.

I also have the privilege of teaching for the INSTEP course in Cambridge, which is a programme connected to, among other places, such distinguished US institutions such as Wake Forest and Tulane universities along with several equally eminent colleges and universities who also enable their students to spend a semester abroad studying history and other subjects in Cambridge every year. The courses are run by the internationally legendary couple Professor Geoffrey Williams and his wife Janice, and over the decades hundreds of American students have had cause to be grateful to them, along with the faculty that the Williams have put together.

I have also benefited considerably from the facilities of the University Library in Cambridge, and of the International Institute for Strategic Studies in London, as well as from the seminar founded by Professor Christopher Andrew (of Cambridge, along with his colleague Peter Martland).

In the past, I taught international relations and Cold War history for various study abroad programmes some of whose students have had links with World War II that gave an added interest to teaching them. I am grateful to the Cardamone family of Sao Paolo whose relative Boagernes Couto Cesar fought in Italy alongside the British and Polish forces, and to the Fabris, Valle, Marchesini and Feitosa/Goyanna families as well.

I am most grateful to the other dedicatees of this book: my wife's Uncle Woody (Woodall Okuykendall Berry Jr) who served as chief crew in Europe during World War II, and to his daughter Ernestine Smith for helping him to come back to where he served some sixty years later, and to my wife's Uncle Lacy (Lacy Foster Paulette Jr) who served in the Battle of the Bulge and who spent his sister's wedding day in a little boat crossing the English channel to Normandy.

My uncle Alan Clough won the MC in Italy during the war. Long-time old friend Geoffrey Drinkwater was one of the intrepid Royal Navy convoy officers who braved the Arctic to take supplies from the USA to the USSR and his courage was finally rewarded in 2013 by a seriously overdue Arctic Medal.

Friends have been of special help in getting this book finished: my wife Paulette and I are profoundly thankful to Andrew and Clare Whittaker, Richard and Sally Reynolds, Lamar and Betsy Weaver, Claude and Leigh Marshall, Larry and Beth Adams, Alasdair and Rachel Paine and Nathan and Debbie Buttery and to their families as well.

I am as always more than grateful to my parents, Frederick and Elizabeth Catherwood, who lived here in Britain throughout the war, and, in my mother's case, survived the Blitz in London as well. All of them lost many friends during the war, and we should never forget the suffering both of those on active service and those civilians still nonetheless on the front line during those terrible six years, and the huge sacrifices that their generation made so that ours can today live in freedom.

Christopher Catherwood
Cambridge, January 2014

Index